Writing Reasons

A Handbook for Judges

EDWARD BERRY

Second Edition

Victoria • British Columbia

Canadian Cataloguing in Publication Data

Berry, Edward, 1940-
    Writing reasons

        Includes bibliographical references.
        ISBN 0-9684309-0-2

        1. Legal composition. 2. Judgments. I. Title.
K94.B47 1998   808'.06634   C98-910940-2

Published by
E-M PRESS
1912 Woodley Road
Victoria, BC V8P 1K3 Canada

Printed in Canada by
MORRISS PRINTING COMPANY LTD.
Victoria, British Columbia

Contents

PREFACE

This handbook was conceived as a follow-up to workshops on judgment writing. The "gentle reader" I envisaged as I began writing was someone I had met, worked with, and learned from. The tone I adopted was therefore conversational. As the writing evolved, however, my aspirations grew—O the arrogance of authors!—and I now believe that the work has something to offer even those judges who have not shared the experience of a workshop. I hope that such readers will also be "gentle" and will imagine themselves part of an ongoing dialogue. Like the workshops that inspired it, the handbook asks judges to think about judgment writing through the eyes of a mere English professor whose knowledge of the law extends no farther than the trial scene of *The Merchant of Venice*. It asks its readers, in short, to make judgments: to accept, adapt or reject suggestions as they do or do not conform to the specific requirements of individual cases and the law.

The handbook reviews the basic principles of judgment writing and includes a series of exercises designed to translate those principles into practice. An appendix provides a key to the exercises, or, more precisely, one of many ways to open the door. The "answers" provided are put forward in the firm expectation that readers will find them inferior to their own. The aim is to keep the conversation going.

Throughout the handbook most of the examples originate from actual judgments. Although I have tried to stay close to the originals—I find them more interestingly difficult than academic concoctions—I have occasionally revised them to heighten a particular problem or point. In all cases that might cause offence, either to parties or authors, I have attempted to render the cases unidentifiable by withholding the name of the author and changing such information as names, dates, and places.

This second edition of *Writing Reasons* reprints the first, with a few corrections and minor revisions.

The "only begetter" of Shakespeare's sonnets was a certain W. H., whose name remains mysterious. This handbook has had many begetters. The most immediate is the Ontario Court of Justice, to which I am much indebted both for financial and moral support. I should like to thank in particular former Chief Judge Sidney B. Linden and Chief Justice Brian W. Lennox for their commitment to the project; the Honourable Justices

Donald Fraser and David A. Fairgrieve for their invaluable advice; Associate Chief Justice J. David Wake for his ongoing support; and the many other judges of that court whose enthusiasm in workshops, even on weekends, has fueled my own.

I am indebted as well to a host of mentors and colleagues associated with the annual program in judgment writing run by the Canadian Institute for the Administration of Justice. Among the professors, I must thank especially Drs. James C. Raymond, John P. Warnock, Jay B. Ludwig, and Harold H. Kolb, Jr. for lectures so inspiring that by now I consider them my own; I hope they will find me at least a faithful and entertaining parrot. Thanks are due as well to Drs. Greig E. Henderson and Judith Herz for sharing ideas and materials. Among my many judicial teachers, I must single out the Honourable Justices Henry E. Hutcheon, James D. Carnwath, and William A. Stevenson. I owe thanks as well to my many so-called students—the Canadian judges whose zestful commitment to good writing and tolerance of English professors has made wrestling with judicial prose not only instructive but fun.

For their generous support in the development of writing workshops, my thanks go to the Honourable Justices Ross Collver and Douglas R. Campbell, and the Honourable Judge Jean Lytwyn.

Finally, for their helpful advice and encouragement in extending the reach of this book to members of administrative tribunals, I must thank Nitya Iyer and Judith Williamson.

I have only myself to thank, alas, for the verbal infelicities and legal blunders that will doubtless amuse this sage readership.

Why Write Judgments?

"Good sentences, and well pronounc'd"
Merchant of Venice, 1.2.10

Why Write Judgments?

"Give your judgments, but give no reasons," Lord Mansfield advised a young justice of the peace in 1799. "As you are a man of integrity, sound sense, and information, it is more than an even chance that your judgments will be right; but, as you are ignorant of the law, it is ten to one that your reasons will be wrong." To *do* justice one need not give reasons; to give them is to take risks. Contemporary judges are expected not only to make but to justify their decisions.

The tension between doing justice and giving reasons is captured provocatively in a quotation from Lord Macmillan. "The main object of a judgment," he said, "is not only to do but to seem to do justice." From this perspective reasons for judgment have to do with seeming. This does not mean that they are a form of pretense, a smoke-screen for caprice or prejudice. It does mean, however, that their function is both logical and psychological. One gives reasons to persuade readers that justice has been done. The writing of judgments, therefore, is an art of persuasion.

Some judges, I find, balk at the idea that judgment writing is persuasive writing. "I don't try to persuade anybody in my judgments," one judge volunteered. "I do justice. Persuasion is for counsel to worry about." This is a reasonable response. Persuasion is a slippery concept, with connotations that link it not only to the courtroom tactics of counsel but to slick rhetoric and the sly deceptions of advertising and public relations. The notion can be applied to judges, however, if we anchor it to argument. If judgments are to persuade, they should do so through the force of effective legal reasoning; they provide *reasons* for judgment. Rhetoric is important to judgment writing not because it clouds reason but because it clarifies it.

Persuasion of any kind, legitimate or illegitimate, requires an understanding of one's audience. For whom is one writing? This is one of the most difficult questions in judgment writing, and one of the questions that makes the genre more difficult than most other kinds. As a Shakespearean,

I write almost exclusively for other scholars of Shakespeare and advanced students. My readership is a tightly knit community with shared assumptions and interests. As a judge, you write for audiences that change often and are potentially unlimited. On some occasions, you may write for the accused; on some, for counsel; on some, for the Court of Appeal. As you write some judgments, a single reader—a particular witness, say— may leap into your consciousness for a paragraph or two and then disappear. Long after writing a judgment, you may find yourself quoted by readers you never contemplated: readers of newspapers, law students, government bureaucrats, even English professors. Few writers have such volatile and shifting audiences.

What is a writer to do in such a situation? Let me try a few general suggestions, which will be amplified and, I hope, justified as the argument of this handbook unfolds. First, never lose sight of the fact that you have an audience. It is easy to forget the existence of readers, especially when you are struggling to keep all of the details of a case under control. Second, never write for an audience of lawyers; write for the human being within the lawyer (be an optimist). Third, aim to reach the educated non-specialist, knowing that at some points, which are surprisingly rare, you may have to narrow your audience. If you write for a lay audience, you may easily shift gears to admit legal technicalities; if you write for lawyers, you will remain trapped forever in legalese. Fourth, remember the distinctive needs of the losing party. Behind each of these suggestions lies an aspiration voiced powerfully in a 1981 address by former Chief Justice Brian Dickson: "Our judgments touch the lives of all Canadians. They should convey meaning to all who read them, whether or not they are learned in the law." The word "our" in that quotation includes the judiciary as a whole.

If, then, the goal of judgments is to persuade educated non-specialists that justice has been done, how is that to be achieved? By focusing on the essential needs of such audiences: clarity, conciseness, and coherence. "Three little words," as the song goes, but big enough to carry us through every chapter of this book.

Why *Write* Judgments?

Readers of this handbook who, for good reasons, spend most of their time delivering oral rather than written judgments might question the usefulness of a handbook devoted to writing. Let me suggest three reasons why attention to the craft of writing might be helpful even for such readers.

The first and most obvious reason is that a judge can never know when a particular case might be so complicated and important as to virtually require written reasons. If effective writing is crucial even on occasion, then it should be taken seriously.

A second reason is that even many so-called oral judgments involve writing. If you reserve judgment for thirty minutes in order to draft reasons to be delivered orally, you are engaged in writing, no matter how primitive the kind. The same is true if you deliver oral reasons without a pause from a draft or outline that you have prepared while listening to the case. Even "true" oral judgments, given extemporaneously without notes, are sometimes likely to reappear in written form as transcripts, like wandering ghosts of prose, returning to haunt their murderers.

A third and final reason for thinking about writing is that, despite their obvious differences, oral and written communication share the same underlying principles. Clarity, conciseness, coherence—these are the essentials of an effective judgment, and the methods of achieving them differ little whether the medium is speaking or writing. In most cases, therefore, the suggestions and exercises provided in this handbook can be readily adapted to oral judgments. Although I shall be writing about writing throughout, I hope that readers with special interests in the oral process will be able to extend the general principles accordingly. To think about writing is to think about communication, a process that affects every judgment, no matter how routine.

A cautionary note, however. Oral judgments are justified, one might say, because they prevent suicides of the kind that Hamlet envisages when he frets about the "law's delay." Oral judgments give us speedy justice. As everyone who has read the transcript of an oral judgment knows, however, the price for express service is often high—so high that we might sometimes be tempted to add motives to Hamlet's suicide list, such as, perhaps, the "law's haste" or the "judge's prose." The faults common to judgment writing—obscurity, wordiness, poor organization—are all accentuated in oral form.

All effective communication, spoken or written, requires thinking, planning, and revising; hence the difficulty of achieving excellence in truly extemporaneous pronouncements. To improve the oral process, one must somehow telescope these three overlapping stages into a very brief time. Some judges have found that through careful note-taking and analysis they can think, plan, and revise as the trial itself unfolds. Others have found that an adjournment of even fifteen or twenty minutes at the end of a trial can achieve remarkable results. Judges who seek to apply the lessons of this handbook to the oral process, therefore, must consider how they can adapt their courtroom practice to the needs of their audiences. The trick is to balance two competing needs: the need for speedy justice and the need for clear reasons.

CHAPTER 1

Introductions

"That is the true beginning of our end"
A Midsummer Night's Dream, 5.1.111

Yes because he never did a thing like that before as ask to get his break-
fast in bed with a couple of eggs since the *City Arms* hotel when he used to
be pretending to be laid up with a sick voice doing his highness to made
himself interesting to that old faggot Mrs Riordan that he thought he had
a great leg of and she never left us a farthing all for masses for herself and
her soul greatest miser ever was actually afraid to lay out 4d for her methy-
lated spirit telling me all her ailments she had too much old chat in her
about politics and earthquakes and the end of the world let us have a bit of
fun first. . . .

By now, unless you are an avid Joycean, you are thoroughly confused.
You thought this handbook was about judgment writing, and this chapter
about introductions.

Let's pause a moment to consider the source of your confusion. The
main problem is that of betrayed expectations. How did your expectations
arise? You first decided to spend some time thinking about judgment writing. You then opened a book entitled *Writing Reasons.* You arrived at a
chapter entitled *Introductions.* And then what? You read an introductory
paragraph, yes, but it happened to be part of Molly Bloom's bedtime monologue from Joyce's *Ulysses.* And without quotation marks.

Consider the different reaction you might have had to this passage if
you were taking a course in twentieth-century fiction. You would know at
the outset that you were reading a novel by James Joyce. You would probably know a certain amount about Joyce to begin with—that he was Irish,
that he was an experimental writer, perhaps even that he invented, or at
least popularized, the distinctively modernist technique of stream-of-consciousness. By the time you encountered this passage, which is in the last
chapter of *Ulysses,* you would have been exposed to more than 500 pages of
the novel. You would know a good deal about the character speaking, and
you would know to expect an experimental technique. You would also know
that you were going to be confused for a while, and that this was part of the
purpose of the work, part of its fun and part of its meaning. You were to be

invited into the process of consciousness itself, invited to follow its meanderings and discover its secret meanings. You were embarked on a voyage of discovery.

The problem with much judgment writing is that it too betrays expectations. One sometimes starts a judgment expecting to find reasons for judgment and discovers instead the judicial counterpart to Molly Bloom's monologue. It is no compliment to be told that you write like James Joyce if you write like Joyce imitating Molly Bloom thinking. Not that there is anything wrong with thinking as Molly Bloom thinks. We all think that way. We all meander from one line of thought to another, flashing from image to idea, moving from past to future to present, circling around and around the anxieties of the moment, and then we go to sleep. If we write like this, however, or speak like this in a courtroom, it is not we who will go to sleep.

The fun of reading Molly Bloom's monologue lies in mapping the terrain as we meander. The fun of reading judgments (if that is not an oxymoron) lies in recognizing the terrain with a map in our hand. Too often judgments make us wander with Molly Bloom.

Here is the beginning of an oral judgment:

> Charles Purdue is charged that on or about the 19th day of October, 1987 at the Municipality of Metropolitan Weston, while his ability to operate a motor vehicle was impaired by alcohol or a drug, operated a motor vehicle contrary to Section 253(a) of the Criminal Code, and that he on the same day in the same place operated a motor vehicle having consumed alcohol in such a quantity that the concentration thereof in his blood exceeded eighty milligrams of alcohol in one hundred millilitres of blood, contrary to Section 253(b) of the Criminal Code. The Crown's evidence consisted of the evidence of the arresting officer, P.C. Meredith and before the trial started Defence and Crown came to the conclusion that jurisdiction, identification, and rights to counsel were not an issue, but the only issue in the case was with regard to first the over eighty charge, which I will deal with first, whether or not the certificate of analysis is admissible based on the argument that the tests were not taken fifteen minutes apart as required by Section 258(1)(c) of the Criminal Code.

What has this passage in common with Molly Bloom's? Both passages bear the hallmarks of thinking aloud. As the paragraph above unfolds, we can observe the judge skimming the charge, recollecting the issues (and the non-issues), and struggling to decide how best to begin. We are voyeurs, in short, observing thought in action. The closer one gets to an extemporaneous oral judgment—the kind that is delivered without pause at the end of a case—the closer one gets to stream-of-consciousness. One witty judge observed that he never gave his conclusion at the outset of an oral judgment because then he could not change his mind en route. When we're in a hurry, we sometimes leave home without a map, hoping that we'll discover our direction as we go.

The metaphor of discovery is apt, for it suggests an important truth about the writing process—that writing (or speaking) can be a means of discovering what we think. A common experience illustrates this notion. You wrestle deeply over a conceptual problem in vain; you then decide to try the problem on a colleague; you reach the half-way point in explaining the problem to her; before she can reply, a light bulb suddenly goes off; you thank your colleague for providing the answer; and you get back to work. The novelist E. M. Forster captured the meaning of this experience well: "how do I know what I think," he asked, "until I hear what I say?" This is the same point a judge made, unknowingly, when asked why the issues of a particular case had not appeared until page thirteen. His reply? "But I didn't know what the issues were myself until I got to page thirteen." Stream-of-consciousness writing is thinking aloud, thinking on paper. It has a very important purpose, and is indeed the way in which much real thinking gets done. But it must not be confused with delivering reasons, with communicating. Hence the need for revision. Only through a second look can we make the transition from writing as discovery of reasons to writing as delivery of reasons.

True stream-of-consciousness writing does not appear very often in written judgments. But other symptoms of the confusion between discovery and delivery are easy to find. One of the most common occurs in the opening paragraphs of judgments. Consider, for example, the opening of a typical provincial court judgment:

> The accused, Mr. Bruce Forman, is charged with possession of a narcotic.
>
> On June 14, 1990, at about 7:00 p.m., Constable Reisbach was in uniform driving a marked cruiser and Constable Sandstrom was his passenger. The accused, driving a 1988 red Toyota van, was stopped at a light northbound at Sussex Road preparing to make a right turn to go westbound on Surrey Drive to visit a friend in a cottage two kilometres away. Surrey Drive is at this point two lanes westbound and two lanes eastbound. Constable Reisbach and Constable Sandstrom watched the accused as he turned onto Surrey Drive. They followed him as he then turned northbound onto Essex Road and stayed behind him until he entered the driveway at 1474 Essex Road. By then it was about 7: 21 p.m.

Because it is typical, many readers will find nothing wrong with this introduction. The context, we might say, is clear: we know we are reading a judgment, we know the nature of the case, and we know that in order to understand the outcome we will have to understand the facts. This is not stream-of-consciousness. The author is not embarked on a voyage of discovery.

The problem, however, whether we are a lay reader or one learned in the law, is that the most important context has been left out: what is the case all about? what are the issues that must be decided? If we are a habitual reader of judgments, we might reply that the statement of issues is bound to appear *after* the treatment of the facts. The hard-core readers of judgments, however, know that this is not always the case: sometimes the issues slide in and out of prominence as the argument unfolds, sometimes they are left to be inferred. Even if they do appear after the facts, however, as readers we need them *before*.

This point becomes immediately clear if we return to the quotation and ask ourselves which facts are crucial to the determination of this case. Is it important that the car was red, or a Toyota, or a van? Do we have to remember that the accused traveled from Sussex Road to Surrey Drive to Essex Road? Is it important that the time of arrival was about 7:21 p.m., not 7:30 p.m.? The vertigo induced by such questions gets worse the longer the narrative of facts goes on, and five or six pages of narrative in such cases is by no means uncommon. By the end of six pages of narrative we may start to feel as if we are in Molly Bloom's mind again. As readers, we find ourselves struggling along without a map, guessing at our ultimate destination as we go along. Which of these many facts will be crucial to the issue or issues we try desperately to infer from them?

Why do judges write like this? Mainly for two reasons, I suspect. First, imitation: judges learn to write judgments in the same way they decide cases, by precedent. Second, courtroom logic: the organization of the judgment follows the way in which most cases are presented—first, the particulars, then the issues that emerge from those particulars. Whatever the ultimate reasons, the result is a method of judgment writing that follows the logic of legal thought but not the needs of an audience. If you have already made a voyage of discovery and your purpose is to show us the way, you need not—indeed, must not—make us retrace your steps. We don't want to climb every mountain of facts you climbed in vain, or enter every tangled thicket of legal argument that led you astray. Your job is to hack us a straight path through the bush to the final destination.

What a reader needs at the beginning of a judgment is a clear map for the journey, a map that includes three things: the nature of the case, the parties involved, and the issue or issues to be decided. Only after these have been established should we be subjected to the facts. Once the issues are clear, both to the author and the reader, the rest of the judgment is generally clear sailing.

Let me illustrate this point with a revised version of the introduction we have just considered:

> The accused, Mr. Bruce Forman, is charged with possession of a narcotic. The accused argues that his detention was arbitrary, that his search

was unlawful and unreasonable, and that the police planted the narcotic on him.

On June 14, 1990, at about 7:00 p.m., Constable Reisbach was in uniform driving a marked cruiser and Constable Sandstrom was his passenger. The accused, driving a 1988 red Toyota van, was stopped at a light northbound at Sussex Road preparing to make a right turn to go westbound on Surrey Drive to visit a friend in a cottage two kilometres away. Surrey Drive is at this point two lanes westbound and two lanes eastbound. Constable Reisbach and Constable Sandstrom watched the accused as he turned onto Surrey Drive. They followed him as he then turned northbound onto Essex Road and stayed behind him until he entered the driveway at 1474 Essex Road. By then it was about 7:21 p.m.

In one sense, very little has changed. The nature of the case, the parties involved—they were already included in the original. The addition consists of a single sentence—a sentence that might have appeared at a later point in the original judgment. The addition of this sentence, however, or its re-positioning, makes all the difference. The three arguments of the accused provide a context for the judgment as a whole. Within that context the facts of the case take on significance. We now know the facts to keep our eye on (and, in many judgments, the facts that might easily have been omitted, like that red Toyota van).

To summarize, then, at the beginning of a judgment readers need above all a clear context. Generally, this context will include the nature of the case, the parties involved, and the issue or issues to be decided. In short and uncomplicated judgments this context can be established within a single paragraph. In long and complicated judgments, especially those with wide and varied audiences, several pages may be necessary. But introductions are introductions, no matter what their length. And they all must serve the same purpose, to orient. As one judge put it after taking a judgment writing course, "the only thing you need to know about judgment writing is to put the issue up front and as little as possible thereafter."

The orientation that takes place in an introduction is not restricted to the nature of the case, the parties, and the issue or issues. Readers are also oriented by being given an argumentative structure, so they know not only the issue but the method that is to be followed. In the above example, we know that each argument of the accused will be dealt with in order. Hence introductions have a crucial role to play in establishing an overall structure.

The point made in the preceding paragraphs may sound like a formula. And in one sense it is. Judgment writing is a restricted genre, and we must expect to find most judgments following similar patterns. Nonetheless, variations are possible and sometimes desirable, depending on the nature of the case. Let's consider one variation. Suppose we add one more sentence at the end of the first paragraph quoted above:

> The accused, Mr. Bruce Forman, is charged with possession of a narcotic. The accused argues that his detention was arbitrary, that his search was unlawful and unreasonable, and that the police planted the narcotic on him. I agree.

Another simple addition, but one with a powerful, and perhaps controversial, effect. If we are looking for a formula, should this addition be part of it? Should introductions not only state the issues but also reveal how they have been decided?

The question is more complicated than might appear at first glance. There are good reasons for revealing the decision at the outset. To do so, for example, flows logically from the needs of readers to have a clear context. If readers need a statement of the issue, then it follows that they will be aided by a statement of how the issue is resolved: that, after all, is the ultimate context. The reasons for judgment can then unfold in the context of the decision. We desire clarity, and what could be clearer?

But there are also good reasons in the opposite direction. To produce the verdict at the outset, for example, may induce the reader, especially the unhappy reader, to stop reading, or at least to continue with mere cynicism. To read the conclusions before the reasons might make the reasons appear to be not reasons at all but mere rationalizations, afterthoughts produced to justify a verdict arrived at by mere prejudice. Surely, one might think, this judge made up her mind in advance.

The question becomes even more complicated if applied to oral judgments. Some judges argue that the losing parties will stop listening if the decision is put up front, others that the parties will not listen unless it *is* put up front. Some argue that the method works well in criminal cases, others that it should never be used in criminal cases. One judge observed that the only sure consequence of beginning with a conclusion is the annoyance of counsel, who, upon receiving a judgment, flip automatically to the last page.

One response to this issue is to dismiss it as trivial: who cares whether a judgment begins or ends with the disposition of the case, as long as the job gets done? This is a reasonable response. It helps to show that judgment writing is not formulaic, that there are decisions to make about how one organizes a judgment, and that these decisions might vary from person to person and case to case. For the sake of clarity, the only important point is that the issues appear at the beginning. Still, the question is not exactly trivial. It shows us, for one thing, that judgment writing involves not merely legal logic but psycho-logic. To think about writing as delivery, not merely discovery, is to think about its effect on an audience. Effects, we might say, are unpredictable. But so are earthquakes, and we do what we can to detect and prepare for them. To imagine stating your conclusion at the outset in different cases and before different audiences is to increase your sensitivity to the psychology of writing.

To test further the possibility for variations in introductions, let's consider four different ways of organizing the same materials. All of the examples below meet the basic test of an introduction: they include the nature of the case, the parties, and the issue. The only difference among them is the position of these three elements. The first example moves from charge to narrative to issue; the second from charge to issue to narrative; the third from narrative to charge to issue; the fourth from issue to charge to narrative. Which version meets most effectively a reader's need for a clear context? Which do you prefer?

(1) Charge-Narrative-Issue

Terry Mercer is charged with assaulting Michael Lawrence.

The incident giving rise to the charge occurred at Westbrook Mall in the Borough of Cliffside. Michael and Diana Lawrence were shopping at the mall with two others: Carla Malatesta, the girlfriend of Mr. Mercer, and Cynthia Frame, the sister of Diana Lawrence. While they were in Smith's Delicatessen, Mr. Mercer entered the store to speak with Ms. Malatesta, with whom he had argued earlier in the day. An argument broke out between Mr. Mercer and Ms. Malatesta, which eventually included Mr. and Ms. Lawrence as well. When the group moved to the parking lot, a fight broke out between Mr. Mercer and Mr. Lawrence that ended with Mr. Lawrence in the hospital with a dislocated shoulder.

According to Mr. Lawrence, his injury was the result of a vicious and unprovoked assault; according to Mr. Mercer, it was the result of a consensual fight. The issue is whether Mr. Lawrence's evidence proves Mr. Mercer's guilt beyond a reasonable doubt.

(2) Charge-Issue-Narrative

Terry Mercer is charged with assaulting Michael Lawrence. Mr. Mercer claims, however, that he participated in a consensual fight. The issue is whether Mr. Lawrence's evidence proves Mr. Mercer's guilt beyond a reasonable doubt.

The incident giving rise to the charge occurred at Westbrook Mall in the Borough of Cliffside. Mr. Lawrence and his wife, Diana, were shopping at the mall with two others: Carla Malatesta, the girlfriend of Mr. Mercer, and Cynthia Frame, the sister of Ms. Lawrence. While they were in Smith's Delicatessen, Mr. Mercer entered the store to speak with Ms. Malatesta, with whom he had argued earlier in the day. An argument broke out between Mr. Mercer and Ms. Malatesta, which eventually included Mr. and Ms. Lawrence as well. When the group moved to the parking lot, a fight broke out between Mr. Mercer and Mr. Lawrence that ended with Mr. Lawrence in the hospital with a dislocated shoulder.

(3) Narrative-Charge-Issue

Michael Lawrence and his wife, Diana, were shopping at Westbrook Mall in Cliffside with two others: Carla Malatesta, the girlfriend of Terry Mercer, and Cynthia Frame, the sister of Ms. Lawrence. While they were in Smith's Delicatessen, Mr. Mercer entered the store to speak with Ms. Malatesta, with whom he had argued earlier in the day. An argument broke out between Mr. Mercer and Ms. Malatesta, which eventually included Mr. and Ms. Lawrence as well. When the group moved to the parking lot, a fight broke out between Mr. Mercer and Mr. Lawrence that ended with Mr. Lawrence in the hospital with a dislocated shoulder.

Mr. Mercer is now charged with assault. He argues, however, that the fight was consensual. The issue is whether the evidence of his alleged victim, Mr. Lawrence, proves Mr. Mercer's guilt beyond a reasonable doubt.

(4) Issue-Charge-Narrative

The issue in this case is whether Michael Lawrence's evidence proves Terry Mercer's guilt beyond a reasonable doubt. Mr. Mercer is charged with assaulting Mr. Lawrence. He argues, however, that the two were engaged in a consensual fight.

The incident giving rise to the charge occurred at Westbrook Mall in the Borough of Cliffside. Mr. Lawrence and his wife, Diana, were shopping at the mall with two others: Carla Malatesta, the girlfriend of Mr. Mercer, and Cynthia Frame, the sister of Ms. Lawrence. While they were in Smith's Delicatessen, Mr. Mercer entered the store to speak with Ms. Malatesta, with whom he had argued earlier in the day. An argument broke out between Mr. Mercer and Ms. Malatesta, which eventually included Mr. and Ms. Lawrence as well. When the group moved to the parking lot, a fight broke out between Mr. Mercer and Mr. Lawrence that ended with Mr. Lawrence in the hospital with a dislocated shoulder.

Which of these versions is "correct"? We can find grounds, I think, to defend them all. Let's apply the rule, "context first, details later," to each of them. In doing so we discover that the three elements—charge, issue, narrative—are each capable of providing a context for the others; each, therefore, can be justified in the first position. To complicate matters further, the ensemble of the three elements can be said to provide the context for the judgment as a whole; this is why it is called an introduction. In defending any of the versions above, we are driven to defend the usefulness of a particular kind of context. The defences would vary from author to author, reader to reader, and case to case. Counsel, for example, might incline towards the first version, moving from charge to narrative to issue; English professors, who like stories, might favour the third version, moving from narrative to charge to issue; law professors might prefer the fourth version, moving from issue to charge to narrative. A criminal case might seem more logical one way, a custody case, another.

If we subject these different versions to our basic test for an introduction, we will find that they all meet it: they all provide the nature of the case, the parties, and the issue. They differ only in the order of the elements. We might argue, then, that since each one does the job, the choice is trivial. The choices can be left to personal preference. But personal preference is not the only criterion. Suppose, for example, the fourth version had begun not with a single issue but with a list of fourteen. In such a case, a reader would almost certainly be confused; instead of providing a context, the issues would become meaningless details. Suppose, in contrast, the third version had begun with a narrative that went on not for one paragraph but for seven pages. In such a case, a reader would again be confused, for the facts would drift along without the anchor of a charge or an issue. All of the versions represented, then, are reasonable only because neither the narrative nor the statement of issues is very long. Only in such a situation is the choice of one version over the other left safely to personal taste.

As a confessed English professor, let me make a special appeal for the narrative-first version, the one judges are least likely to prefer. In some cases the most useful opening context is who did what to whom. A story captures attention and focuses the mind. And although audiences for judgments are usually captive audiences, it does no harm to arouse their interest.

The main point of all of this, however, is not to provide a formula or to suggest a preference but to highlight the range of options available and the importance of being aware of them. Effective writing consists of knowing the options and selecting them appropriately, according to the nature of the audience, the occasion, and the particular case at hand.

A final word of caution. Meeting the formal requirements does not guarantee an effective introduction. In writing, as in golf, one can make the right moves badly. Consider this example of an opening sentence:

> This is an appeal from the order of Mr. Justice N. P. Harris that there be a *pari passu* distribution between the appellant, The Attorney General of Canada and the respondent, Ralph Forster as judgment creditors, of $47,732.00 of insurance monies paid into Court by the insurers of the defendant judgment debtor Judith Michaels under an owner's motor vehicle liability insurance policy pursuant to s. 320(1) of the *Insurance Act of Alberta* R.S.A. 1980 c.1-5 and amendments.

This opening, we might argue, is well on its way to meeting the requirements of an introduction: it introduces the nature of the case and the parties, and it gestures towards issues that can be developed in the next sentence or two. We *might* argue that way, that is, if we were not thoroughly confused. The problem with this introduction is a common one and springs from the laudable aim of brevity: the author is trying to compress every conceivable detail into a single sentence. To solve the problem in this instance the sentence can be divided, the information can be presented in smaller units, and the technical vocabulary can be reduced or perhaps withheld until a later stage in the argument. Conciseness, in short, must sometimes yield to clarity, especially in introductions.

A final point about introductions. First impressions, we are told, are important. A firm handshake, a welcome expression, eye contact—in our culture, at least, these are the hallmarks of an effective personal introduction. They create an image of the self. And first meetings can be especially important in creating that image. Consider, for example, the differences between two ways of introducing the same judgment. I quote only the first sentence of each version:

> (1) This is an application by the Attorney General of Canada pursuant to section 18.1 of the *Federal Court Act* for an order quashing the decision of the Canadian Human Rights Commission ("Commission"), dated March 17, 1995, referring the complaint of the respondent, Jeremy Li, under the *Canadian Human Rights Act* ("Act") against the National Energy Council ("N.E.C.") to the Canadian Human Rights Tribunal ("Tribunal") for inquiry.

> (2) In 1992, Mr. Jeremy Li filed a complaint with the Canadian Human Rights Commission alleging that his employer, the National Energy Council, discriminated against him contrary to sections 7 and 10 of the Canadian Human Rights Act.

In each of these versions the prose creates an authorial voice. The voice behind the first version is impersonal, technical, driven by the machine of the law; the voice behind the second is personal, non-technical, and driven by the human predicament behind the case. In reality, the author of both versions is the same person; on the page, however, where "the style is the man" or woman, we encounter two persons. We will consider some of the implications of these stylistic choices in Chapter 6.

To summarize. The most important page in a judgment is page one. An effective introduction tells the reader what the judgment is all about and maps out the argumentative terrain. All introductions should include three elements: the nature of the case, the parties involved, and the issue or issues. These elements can be organized in different ways, depending upon the audience, occasion, and materials of the case. An introduction may also (but need not) reveal the decision in the case. Introductions must be clear without being overly precise or technical, and concise without being overly compressed. Effective introductions, like prologues to plays or overtures to operas, not only alert the audience to the ensuing action but keep them in their seats. Like formal introductions in society, introductions to judgments also create an image of the self.

* * *

Exercises: Introductions
Exercise Key, p. 90

A. *Review the following introductions. Identify their main strengths and weaknesses, in relation to the criteria discussed in this chapter.*

1. In the early morning hours of October 20, 1993, the accused, Jimmy Bertie, played his stereo so loudly that it disturbed the peace of mind of his upstairs neighbour, Randolph Murphy, causing the light fixtures in the Murphy residence to shake. The accused not only ignored Mr. Murphy's complaints but also told a police officer investigating the noise to "Fuck Off." The officer arrested Mr. Bertie, who was then charged with committing mischief by interfering with the lawful enjoyment of property contrary to s. 430 of the *Criminal Code*.

    The question for consideration is the meaning of the term "lawful enjoyment of property." Does it mean "freedom from noise or other things that could reduce the quality of life," or is it restricted to a "direct interference with the possessory right of property"?

2. This is an appeal by Douglas College, pursuant to s. 109 of the *Labour Code* R.S.B.C.1979 c.212, from an arbitration award issued August 25, 1986.

    The appeal raises the question of the application of the *Canadian Charter of Rights and Freedoms* and the power of an arbitrator to determine *Charter* issues.

    The collective agreement which governs the relations between Douglas College and its employees, represented by the Faculty Association, contains a provision for mandatory retirement at age 65.

    The Faculty Association brought a grievance, contending that the mandatory retirement provision was inconsistent with s. 15(1) of the *Charter*, and, therefore, of no force and effect. The arbitrator held that s. 32 of the *Charter* applied to the College's relations with its employees, and that the collective agreement was "law" within s. 15(1) of the *Charter*.

    The appellant raises three issues: first, whether the arbitrator erred in concluding that the College was government within s. 32 of the

Charter; second, whether the collective agreement was law; and third, whether the arbitrator was competent to determine those issues.

3. The defendant is an impaired driver. He was convicted for drinking and driving offences seven times between January, 1965 and March, 1987. He now faces sentence for two more convictions by reason of guilty pleas entered July 19, 1988 to charges arising from incidents in February and April of this year. They bring to five the number of occurrences discovered since September, 1978. Against this background the matter of sentence should be relatively simple, but it is complicated here by the provisions of s. 255(5) of the *Criminal Code*, which the defendant invokes to apply for conditional discharges on the latest two offences.

4. On February 23, 1994, at approximately 1:00 a.m., Bruce Edwin Callins will be executed by the State of Texas. Intravenous tubes attached to his arms will carry the instrument of death, a toxic fluid designed specifically for the purpose of killing human beings. The witnesses, standing a few feet away, will behold Callins, no longer a defendant, an appellant or a petitioner, but a man, strapped to a gurney, and seconds away from extinction.

    Within days, or perhaps hours, the memory of Callins will begin to fade. The wheels of justice will churn again, and somewhere, another jury or another judge will have the unenviable task of determining whether some human being is to live or die.

5. This is an appeal and a cross-appeal from the order of a Motions Judge in the Trial Division pronounced on January 13, 1989, which dismissed a motion by the Respondent (Appellant by cross-appeal) for a declaration that the Appellant (Respondent by cross-appeal) must, in calculating the Respondent's statutory release date, take into account and credit to the unexpired portion of the Respondent's sentence the earned remission standing to his credit on November 1, 1988.

6. Mr. Deeble has a milk round. He sells milk to people at the doors of their houses. He runs his business from a dairy building where he keeps his equipment, refrigerator, spare milk bottles, and so forth and a stable where he keeps his horse and float. His round is seven streets adjoining the premises. He does not actually have a shop as ordinarily understood. His lease of these premises is coming to an end, and he wants to stay on there. This depends on whether the premises come within the definition of a "shop" in the *Leasehold Property Act*.

B. *Use the information provided below to write four versions of an introduction, following the models discussed in this chapter: (1) charge-narrative-issue (2) charge-issue-narrative (3) narrative-charge-issue (4) issue-charge-narrative. Since the case is not a criminal case, you will have to adapt the model accordingly.*

1. The case: Her Majesty the Queen (Plaintiff) and L.M., Inc.(Defendant), Federal Court of Canada, Trial Division, March 7, 1989.

2. The issue: is a converted tugboat a yacht?

3. The law: Section 18(1)(1) of the *Income Tax Act*, Stats. Can. 1970-71-72, c.63 disallows certain kinds of expenses as deductions in computing a taxpayer's taxable income. The section states:

    > In computing the income of a taxpayer from a business or property no deduction shall be made in respect of:

    > an outlay or expense made . . . for the use or maintenance of property that is a yacht, a camp, a lodge or a golf course. . . .

4. Facts:

    a. The defendant, L.M. Inc., is a corporation engaged in manufacturing tables. L. M. Inc. spent $20,000 in the taxation year of 1985 and $47,000 in the taxation year of 1986 to hire the *Seawind* for the purpose of entertaining guests. The corporation deducted the above amounts from its taxes as business expenses. Revenue Canada argues that the deductions should be disallowed.

    b. The *Seawind* was built in 1947 as a tugboat. It was used as a tugboat until 1981. At that point changes were made to the boat to enable it to serve as the residence of its owners, Mr. and Mrs. Randolph, and as a charter boat for fishing and other recreational purposes. When the changes were completed, the Randolph's sold their home on land and moved into the boat, which they continue to use as their only residence.

    c. The changes made to the boat in 1981 included removal of the winch and conversion of the winch area into a lounge with paneled walls and a carpeted floor.

    d. The *Seawind* is used for fishing charters only six weeks a year, when Mr. Randolph is on vacation from his regular job. It can be chartered for weddings and similar parties on weekends and holidays throughout the year.

21

e. The advertising brochure put out by Mr. and Mrs. Randolph includes the following:

The *Seawind* is ideally suited for sales seminars, private executive meetings or your own special party. It offers accommodation for up to 14 passengers on overnight charters.

The main deck features seven comfortable cabins and a well equipped galley specializing in exotic cuisine. The large and tasteful lounge affords sofas, a piano, and an electric organ for lively evenings.

CHAPTER 2

Organization

"Keep law and form and due proportion"

Richard II, 3.4.41

The Romantic poet Samuel Taylor Coleridge believed that poems should be like trees; their form should be organic, determined only by the inner logic of a seed of inspired thought. Judgments are more like houses than trees and their composition more like carpentry than the growth of a seed. Although the ways in which humans may become entangled in the law seem infinite in number, the forms that the legal process takes are few. Reading judgments is often like a drive through the suburbs of the nineteen-fifties: the colours of the houses may vary, and occasionally the number of rooms, but the basic shape remains the same. Even judges who produce paragraphs that sound like Molly Bloom's monologue usually do so within a traditional, if often poorly marked, argumentative structure.

What is this basic design? Most judgments are organized as follows:

Introduction—nature of the case, parties
Facts
Argument—law in relation to facts
Conclusion—disposition of the case

We have already noticed in Chapter 1 the main problem with this structure: it makes no mention of the issues, which are presumably left to unfold somewhere in the section entitled "Argument." So let's revise this outline to include the issues:

Introduction—nature of the case, parties, issue(s)
Facts
Argument—law in relation to facts for each issue
Conclusion—disposition of the case

One may vary this structure in several ways: the conclusion may appear at the outset; the facts may be many or few and may appear under "Argument" as well as under "Facts"; the section entitled "Argument" may be divided and subdivided, depending upon the number of issues. But judges, unlike Samuel Taylor Coleridge, are unlikely to create a radically new form.

And for good reason. The purpose of judgments is to subject constantly varying situations to the relative stability of the law—to pour new wine, one might say, into old bottles.

Since the structure of judgments is relatively predictable, one often finds it re-enforced by common headings, such as Introduction, Facts, Argument, Conclusion, or Introduction, Undisputed Facts, Disputed Facts, Law, Issues, Conclusion. Although headings are usually unnecessary in short judgments, in long ones they serve several useful purposes. They make it possible for a reader to identify a specific section of interest; they provide structural clarity; and they remove the need for transitional sentences, which are often cumbersome (and often, alas, forgotten by the author). The longer and more complicated the judgment, the more helpful the use of headings.

The headings listed above are what might be called all-purpose headings. Facts, Law, Conclusion—these headings might appear in any kind of judgment. Because they are a kind of boilerplate, they can be mildly dangerous. If such headings become merely habitual, they lull the writer into complacency—headings do not create order but merely re-enforce it. At best, moreover, all-purpose headings provide the reader with only a vague sense of direction: the signpost "Argument" gives us the name of the sub-division but not the address of the house we want to find. The most useful headings, for both reader and writer, are those that are specific to the judgment at hand.

Here is an example of former Chief Justice Dickson's use of specific headings in *Ogg-Moss V. The Queen*:

    I.   Background and Facts
    II.   The Decisions in the Ontario Courts
    III.   The Grounds of Appeal
    IV.   The Purpose and Effect of s.43
    V.   Is a mentally retarded adult a "child" for the purposes of s.43?
        (a) "Child" in s.43 and its common law antecedents
        (b) The "functional' reading of "child"
    VI.   Is a Mental Retardation Counsellor a "Person Standing in the Place of a Parent" to a Mentally Retarded Person Under His Charge?
    VII.   Is the Relationship between a Mental Retardation Counsellor and a Mentally Retarded Adult Under His Care That of "School teacher" and "Pupil"?
        (a) "Pupil"
        (b) "Schoolteacher"
    VIII.   Using Force by Way of Correction
    IX.   Conclusion

[1984] 2 S.C.R.173

Although most provincial court judgments do not require such elaboration, Chief Justice Dickson's practice in *Ogg-Moss* illustrates the virtue of headings that are specific to the case at hand. Such headings provide more than a general sense of direction; they clarify the precise structure of the argument.

Having considered the overall structure of a judgment, let's examine individually the sections in our basic outline: introduction, facts, argument, conclusion. Since we have already dealt with introductions in Chapter 1, we may begin with the facts.

Facts

In my youth I was hooked on a TV show called *Dragnet*. It featured an irresistible theme song (dum-de-dum-dum, dum-de-dum-dum . . . dum) and a tough cop with an irresistible line ("Just the facts, ma'am, just the facts"). I find myself thinking of Joe Friday whenever I think of provincial court judgments.

The facts are the bane of provincial courts. How does one reduce the factual narrative without creating potential problems on appeal? How does one set out the conflicting testimony of seven witnesses who disagree on just about everything? How does one separate findings of fact from mere narrative overview? How does one avoid repeating facts that bear on several different arguments? How does one explain why one witness is more credible than another without resorting to vague statements about demeanour? "Just the facts," indeed!

Dealing with facts will always pose problems, but it helps to keep in mind some of the available options. Let me suggest five:

1. Reduce the statement of facts as much as possible. The only essential facts are those that are necessary to decide the legal questions at hand.

2. Introduce your judgment with a factual overview that clarifies the issue and creates a framework for the more detailed treatment of facts to follow.

3. When the facts are not in dispute, avoid repetition by providing a factual overview, withholding details until they become relevant to the particular issues of the case.

4. When the facts are in dispute, consider the following possibilities:
   a. dividing the undisputed facts from the disputed facts.
   b. narrating the facts as a unit, with occasional interruptions for disputed facts.

5. Keep the reader informed of how you intend to handle the facts and why. When the facts are not in dispute, say so. When they are, indicate the nature of the problem and how you intend to handle it. In short, provide a context before you plunge into the facts.

Argumentative Structure

The word "argument" is interestingly ambiguous. It can mean "quarrel" or it can mean "reasoned demonstration." We owe thanks to the French for the former: in Old French, *arguer* meant "to blame." We owe thanks to the Romans for the latter: in Latin, *arguere* meant "to make clear." Both meanings are relevant to judgments; the purpose of a judgment, one might say, is to clarify quarrels and, in so doing, to resolve them.

The ambiguity of the word highlights the two basic methods of developing the "argument" of a judgment. One method relies on the quarrel. Behind every case is an argument, a dispute between parties. What more natural than to make that dispute the framework for one's treatment of the legal issues? The Crown argues that Willy Jones is guilty of assault; the defence argues that the evidence is insufficient. The Crown argues that John Miles has violated a by-law; the defence argues that he has not done so, and that even if he has, the by-law is unconstitutional. Trials are quarrels, and it makes great sense to put that fact to rhetorical use: it clarifies the issues and assures each party that his or her position has been heard.

In judgments as in life, however, quarrels do not always produce clarity. To rely on them as a structural device may sometimes create problems. On some occasions, for example, the arguments of counsel may distort the issues of the case, threatening the clarity of the judge's own argument; on others, the arguments of counsel may be irrelevant, forcing the judge to waste words and time. Once one is embarked on retracing the arguments of counsel as a means of structuring a judgment, wordiness is difficult to resist; unless one is careful, the voices of counsel take over the judgment and the overall argument—*your* argument—may lose its shape. The alternative to this method is for the judge to take control, to define and develop the issues in the manner that is most likely to persuade, and to use the arguments of counsel only when they bear directly on the issues.

The two alternatives can be seen in the following examples of introductory paragraphs:

Argument as Quarrel

The Appellants, a contractor and a worker, were convicted of violating the *Occupational Health and Safety Act* (the *Act*) by operating machinery within three metres of an energized power line. Each was fined $500.

The Crown argues that the power line was energized to the levels required by the *Act*, and that the exemptions within the *Act* do not apply to the Appellants. The Appellants, in contrast, contend that the evidence is insufficient to show that the line was energized to the required levels and that, even if were sufficient, exemptions within the *Act* apply to their actions.

The Appellants, a contractor and a worker, were convicted of violating the *Occupational Health and Safety Act* (the *Act*) by operating machinery within three metres of an energized power line. Each was fined $500.

The issues in this appeal are (1) whether the power line was energized to the levels required by the *Act*, and (2) if so, whether the actions of the Appellants fall within exemptions provided by the *Act*.

While each of the above versions is reasonably clear and concise, the former takes more words than the latter, highlighting what can easily happen to a judgment based on the "Argument as Quarrel" method. Often, as in the example immediately above, the positions of both parties become obvious upon a clear statement of the issues.

The Order of an Argument

Legal arguments, one hopes, are governed by legal logic. The steps by which an argument unfolds, therefore, are dictated by the legal tests that must be applied. Which issue is to be dealt with first, then, and which second or third, is usually not a matter of choice. To argue the case quoted above, for example, one must begin with the issue of the energy level of the power line, for if the Crown's claim on that point is not proved beyond a reasonable doubt, the case is dismissed; whether the Appellants' actions might be excused by exemptions in the *Act* becomes then an idle question.

The first question to ask in structuring an argument, then, is the order of the argument, and the order is often a forgone conclusion. The law has its own remorseless logic. When structural problems occur in judgments, they usually occur not because a legal argument has been poorly made but because it has been poorly marked. The problem is especially acute for readers who are not lawyers. The argumentative moves in a typical judgment—a case of shoplifting, say, or a case about parental custody for a child—are so familiar to most judges and lawyers that the structure tying them together is often scarcely visible. For the lay reader, however, our "preferred" audience, clarity requires that the structure be laid bare. Even lawyers, moreover, like portrait painters, may find it helpful to think of the skeleton beneath the flesh.

Hence the usefulness of headings, which, if used specifically, give us the bones of an argument. But what happens when the judgment is too short and simple for headings? And what happens *within* headings, when a particular issue requires lengthy explanation and argument, as when, to cite *Ogg-Moss*, we must decide whether we may consider "a mentally retarded adult a 'child' for the purposes of s.43?" In such cases readers need occasional signposts: reminders of where they have been and anticipations of where they are to go.

The most important signpost for a judgment, as we saw in Chapter 1, is the introductory statement of the issue or issues. Suppose we encounter the following on the second page of a decision of the B.C. Court of Appeal:

> The appellant raises three issues: first, whether the arbitrator erred in concluding that the College was government within s.32 of the Charter; second, whether the collective agreement was law; and third, whether the arbitrator was competent to determine those issues.

Having received this information, we know not only the issues but the argumentative structure of the judgment as a whole. We will not be surprised to find headings for each of these issues, in order. Having oriented us in this way at the outset, the writer must now ensure that we remain on track to the end. Readers are like tour groups: they want to be told where they are going, what they are seeing en route, and where they have been— nearly all the time.

The following well-marked paragraphs illustrate, in miniature, the usefulness of transitional signals throughout a judgment:

> The question which we must decide is whether the act of the College in coming to an agreement with the Faculty Association with respect to the terms of the collective agreement is 'law' within s.15(1) of the *Charter*. For the purposes of this case, we need go no further than to define 'law' as comprehending a rule or system of rules formulated by government and imposed upon the whole or a segment of society. In this context, law may be made by government itself or by bodies or agencies exercising governmental power.
>
> Are the provisions of the collective agreement in this case to be regarded as 'law' within s.15(1) of the *Charter*?
>
> Generally the provisions of a collective agreement or a private contract—for instance, those in issue in the *University of British Columbia* case— are not regarded as law. That is because such agreements are usually the result of the will of the contracting parties, and are not imposed by government. Law is not created by negotiation, or by agreement between the parties, even if one of them is government; it is imposed.
>
> In this case, however, the collective agreement does not take effect as a result of the will of the contracting parties. It takes effect only as a result of the decision of the commissioner under the *Compensation Stabilization Act*, in exercise of government power, to impose terms. The fact that the impugned provision depends for its validity upon government approval takes it out of the realm of a privately negotiated agreement and places it in the realm of law, subjecting it to scrutiny under s.15(1) of the *Charter*.

This writer keeps in mind the reader's need for constant orientation. The first paragraph raises the question that must be decided and provides a definition necessary to the question. The second paragraph backtracks, restating the question in summary form (notice how effectively a question mark captures attention). The third paragraph sets out the general rule in collective agreements (notice how the placement of "Generally" as the emphatic first word provides a clue that this case is exceptional). The fourth paragraph confirms what we expected, that this collective agreement falls within the realm of law (notice how the final sentence circles back to the beginning of our short journey, reminding us of s.15(1) of the *Charter*).

Good writers keep the need for orientation in mind in every part of the judgment. And not only good *writers*. Transitions are even more important in extemporaneous oral judgments, where the tendency to meander like Molly Bloom is difficult to avoid. In such situations careful transitions may serve a double purpose, orienting not only the listener but the speaker.

To summarize this section on "Argument":

1. Choose a method of argument that best suits the case. The most obvious are "Argument as Quarrel" and "Argument as Reasoned Demonstration."

2. Choose the most logical order for the elements of the judgment. Use headings to re-enforce the order if the judgment is long and complicated.

3. Keep constantly in mind the reader's need for orientation. Provide a clear statement of the issues at the outset, and provide clear transitions from sentence to sentence, paragraph to paragraph, and section to section.

Conclusions

To the reader, a conclusion should seem both just and inevitable. Having been guided through the jungle of facts, ferried along the treacherous river of the law, and carried up the mountain of legal argument, we now rest happily on the summit of judgment, the whole course of the journey spread out before our eyes, the final resting place now revealed as our only conceivable destination. Justice has triumphed. "Yes," the accused cries out as he reaches page fourteen, "I am guilty. I go happily to jail, knowing that justice has been done."

Except for losing readers, conclusions are not generally a problem in judgments. For the judge, there are few options: guilty or not guilty, custody or no custody, fine or no fine. In *The French Lieutenant's Woman*, the novelist John Fowles provides two different endings, letting his readers decide which one they prefer. The favourite ending of modern art-films is ambiguity: will this tormented couple get back together or not? Multiple choice, ambiguity, ambivalence—these are not among the options available to judges.

Despite the narrow range of options, conclusions to judgments sometimes seem unearned. The way to earn an ending, of course, is to argue patiently and methodically throughout the judgment as a whole. If a conclusion seems unearned, it may *be* unearned. A common symptom of the unearned conclusion is the sweeping assertion, "Having considered all the evidence and reviewed all the authorities provided by counsel, I therefore conclude. . . ." The vagueness of that assertion—and it appears often in judgments—creates resistance in readers, not assurance ("the lady protests too much, methinks," to quote Queen Gertrude in *Hamlet*).

If a judgment is short and the argument crisp and clear, the reader needs nothing more than the conclusion itself: "I therefore find you guilty." If the judgment is long and the argument complicated, a reader needs more than the cloudy assurance that the judge has considered absolutely everything. In such cases, a brief summary might help: "I find you not guilty for the following reasons—1, 2, 3, 4." In certain cases, it might help not only to summarize the reasons but to weigh them: "For three reasons, therefore, I conclude that Sarah's interests are best served in the custody of Mr. Jones: she will be able to continue at her present school; she will be able to visit her mother on a regular basis; and, above all, she will have the continuing support of her paternal grandparents, to whom she is deeply attached." Like tour groups (again), readers find it powerfully reassuring at the end of a journey to recall not only where they have been and what they have seen but what has been most important.

To summarize:

1. Endings must be earned. One cannot end well if one has argued ill.

2. Avoid vague and sweeping assertions about the argumentative process.

3. In short judgments, end without fanfare.

4. In long judgments, consider the virtues of a summary or a weighted summary at the conclusion.

* * *

Exercises: Organization
Exercise Key, p. 93

1. *Organizing the facts—The following judgment deals with a case involving conflicting testimony. It suffers from common problems in clarity, conciseness, and coherence. Without altering its essential nature, revise the judgment, paying particular attention to the handling of the factual narrative and the questions of credibility.*

THE COURT: We are dealing with two charges of assault against George Wilson arising out of events on the 13th of December, 1995 in the City of Warwick. On that date Mr. Wilson attended at a local bar where Louise Mercer was working as a cocktail waitress. He arrived there before four o'clock in the afternoon when she started work and he stayed there until she left work, which was 8:30 p.m. They were social friends up until that date.

The accused was drinking beer. He admits having at least five beer. Ms. Mercer, who served him, testified she served him approximately eight beer. In any event, during the course of the evening Ms. Mercer spoke with the accused with respect to what she perceived to be his inappropriate conduct with an exotic dancer. He became angry and told her to call Bev, who is his wife. Ms. Mercer responded by going to the telephone behind the bar to comply with his request. As she stood there holding the telephone with her left hand, he was leaning over the bar, angry and yelling, and he flicked his cigarette towards her. There is a difference in the evidence with respect to her exact position. She describes her position as holding the phone, leaning against the wall containing the bottles and facing out towards him. He describes her as facing the telephone which was on the wall. In any event, he agrees that he, out of frustration, flicked his cigarette over the bar and that she was standing opposite him. He claims the cigarette hit the bottles behind her. There is a corner to the wall and if he was facing into the corner he could view the bottles as being behind her. She says the cigarette hit her cheek.

The other people who testified who were in the bar describe him leaning over the bar yelling, angry and flicking his cigarette. Ronson, who was the accused's friend, testified that the accused flicked the cigarette in Ms. Mercer's general direction. He says the cigarette did not hit her.

At this time Ms. Mercer was on the telephone with the accused's spouse, Beverly Brown. Ms. Mercer testified that she advised Ms. Brown that he (the accused) had just hit her in the face with a cigarette. Ms. Brown denied hearing of the cigarette event when she was talking to Ms. Mercer on the telephone. She does, however, agree that Ms. Mercer told her on the telephone that Ms. Mercer was going to phone the police concerning the accused's actions. There is no explanation whatsoever as to why she thought Ms. Mercer was going to call the police on her spouse and it makes logical sense that she knew at that point that he had flicked the cigarette towards her. George Athopolis, who lives with Ms. Mercer, described these events at the bar. He saw the accused lean over and flip his cigarette at Ms. Mercer. He did not see if it struck her because somebody intervened in his line of sight. He did describe Ms. Mercer as holding her cheek afterwards, although he demonstrated with his left hand. He then stood beside the accused and he testified that the accused said to him, "Keep your bitch girlfriend in line." He described how the accused then called Ms. Mercer a number of unsavory names to which Ms. Mercer responded that the accused was an alcoholic who did not deserve his beautiful wife and children.

Ms. Mercer left the bar and purchased cigarettes to take to Beverly Brown who had requested that she do so. She spoke with Ms. Brown in the apartment with respect to what had happened at the bar and they heard the accused arrive home. Ms. Mercer mounted the stairs and describes how she met the accused on the narrow landing where he shoved her into a tricycle on the landing. The accused denies this. He testified that he met her on the stairs, not on the landing. He was questioned thoroughly about this and he would have the Court believe that although he saw Ms. Mercer, whom he was concerned about because she had already reported him to the police, coming up the stairs, he did not wait for her to climb to the top of the stairs. Instead, he started down the stairs and they passed on the staircase. Ms. Brown, who was excluded with the other witnesses from the testimony in court, describes the accused meeting Ms. Mercer on the landing. She was tending the four-year-old on the stairs, and she stated she did not see anything happen.

Upon a consideration of the whole of the evidence I am satisfied beyond a reasonable doubt of the accused's guilt with respect to each of these charges. I find as a fact that he was angry with Ms. Mercer when he leaned over the bar and flicked the cigarette at her. Whether it struck her directly or after glancing off the bottles is irrelevant. She was hit by the cigarette. His flicking the cigarette at her when he was angry with her constitutes an assault. I also find as a fact that Ms. Mercer told Ms. Brown about that event on the telephone, otherwise Ms. Brown's admission that she knew that Ms. Mercer was going to call the police on her spouse makes no sense.

With respect to the events at the apartment, the accused is not being forthright and honest with the Court when he denies that he met her on the landing where she says he pushed her. This meeting place is confirmed by Ms. Brown who did not realize the import of this piece of evidence. Ms. Brown was tending the children and, apart from glancing up to see him come in, was not keeping her eye on what he did with respect to Ms. Mercer.

The accused and Ms. Mercer met on the landing and he pushed her into the tricycle. He was intoxicated from drinking for some four hours in the bar. His witness, Athopolis, was not sober. Ms. Mercer was, of course, sober. Ms. Brown was in the unenviable position of trying to help out the accused with whom she lives and has children.

There will be a finding of guilty with respect to each of the charges.

2. *Organizing an argument—The following excerpt is taken from a judgment that hinges on whether the evidence of a breathalyzer test should be admissible when the roadside screening test that preceded it was administered improperly. Roadside screening tests must be conducted immediately; in this case the accused was required to wait about 20 minutes for the police to locate the screening device. Counsel for the defence argued that admitting the evidence would bring the administration of justice into disrepute. The excerpt deals only with the issues involved in determining whether the admission of such evidence would bring the administration of justice into disrepute.*

   Revise the excerpt, paying particular attention to its overall organization.

As a trial judge, I must consider whether the admission of the evidence would bring the administration of justice into disrepute. The factors to be considered are the fairness of the trial, the seriousness of the *Canadian Charter of Rights and Freedoms* violation and, if the breach can be characterized as trivial, whether it would bring the administration of justice into disrepute if the evidence were admitted.

It is clear that the exclusion of evidence of breathalyzer readings is not automatic once an infringement of an accused's constitutional rights in the course of obtaining the evidence is established. In order to have evidence excluded, the accused must establish in light of all the circumstances of the case, the admission of the evidence in the proceedings would bring the administration of justice into disrepute. Each case must be determined on its own facts.

Beginning with *R. v. Collins* 33 C.C.C. (3d) 1, the Supreme Court of Canada has developed the framework for a s. 24(2) analysis which separates the various relevant factors into three categories for consideration. Those three factors are the fairness of the trial, the seriousness of the violation and the effect on the repute of the administration of justice of excluding the evidence.

The concept of trial fairness which is invoked in s. 24(2) in a 24(2) analysis, embodies a broad right against self-incrimination in the sense of a right not to be conscripted by the State in the process of building a case against oneself. The Supreme Court of Canada has drawn a distinction between real evidence and self-incriminatory evidence. The distinction is important because the Supreme Court has consistently held that the omission of real evidence following a breach will generally not adversely affect the fairness of the trial, whereas the admission of self-incriminatory evidence will.

Self-incriminatory evidence includes not only statements made by an accused but also evidence obtained with the compelled assistance of the accused, such as breath and blood samples. Because the evidence in issue in the case at bar is self-incriminatory evidence, concerns with respect to the fairness of the trial are central to the s. 24(2) analysis.

In *R. v. Elshaw* (1991) 67 C.C.C. (3d) 97, at page 129, Justice Iacobucci, on behalf of the court, stated that it was an error to consider the self-incriminatory nature of evidence as merely one factor among many to be taken into account in a s. 24(2) analysis. Rather, he stated, as a general rule, such evidence is not admissible because it would adversely affect the fairness of the trial and bring the administration of justice into disrepute.

The question, however, that must still be asked in every case is whether, in the particular circumstances presented, would the fairness of the trial be adversely affected by the admission of the evidence.

In accordance with my analysis, I have determined that while the reading of the samples of breath taken pursuant to s. 254(2) was not evidence that went to the guilt or innocence of the accused, it was a key factor that could properly be characterized as the linchpin to the right to demand that the accused provide a breath sample pursuant to s. 254(3).

Furthermore, while I do not wish to describe the actions of this particular police officer as being in bad faith as he was following what I perceive to be an accepted practice, the approach used in the case at bar, in my opinion, represents a practice adopted by the local police force that I would characterize as a ruse designed to circumvent the true spirit of the legislation.

In the circumstances, I am satisfied that to admit the evidence would render the trial unfair.

In conclusion, I am satisfied that the accused has met the onus of establishing that to admit the breathalyzer results would have put the administration of justice into disrepute in the eyes of a reasonable person, dispassionate and fully apprised of the circumstances of the case. Accordingly, the breathalyzer results will be excluded from evidence in this trial and, as a result, the accused is acquitted.

CHAPTER 3

Conciseness

"He draweth out the thread of his verbosity finer than
the staple of his argument"
Love's Labor's Lost, 5.1.16

I have never heard anyone complain that judgments were too short. By definition, it seems, a judgment is a prose argument that is forty percent longer than it needs to be. If we could save forty percent on every judgment, we could save the forests of British Columbia.

Why are judgments too long? One reason is haste. The closer one comes to Molly Bloom's stream-of-consciousness, the more likely one is to be long-winded. The Chinese scholar who apologized to his friend for having written such a long letter had a point: "I'm sorry to have written such a long letter," he wrote, "but I didn't have time for a short one." Conciseness requires revision.

But haste is not the only reason. A more important reason, I suspect, is anxiety. Judges write too much because they fear the consequences of writing too little. The finder of fact worries that one fact too few will require a totally new trial upon appeal; the surveyor of precedent fears that six cited cases will not convince readers accustomed to twelve ; the quoter of contracts worries that the significance of a single clause will be challenged without at least a full page of context.

This is not paranoia. Curtness can get one into trouble. But all effective writing requires selection. If six cases are too few, why stop at twelve? If a clause is too little, why stop at a page? Knowing how to write concise judgments is knowing where to draw the line—or, perhaps, knowing what to draw the line through.

Since the anxieties that produce wordiness are essentially legal rather than rhetorical, they must be resolved case by case by those who do the writing. To work towards conciseness, however, it helps to keep in mind the most common obstacles. Wordiness may afflict all parts of a judgment: sentences, paragraphs, the argument overall. Since we will deal with sentences and paragraphs in a later chapter, let me focus at this point on larger units of thought. What can judges do beyond writing shorter sentences and paragraphs to save the forests of British Columbia? The suggestions below do not encourage clear-cutting, merely ecologically sound management of resources:

1. Prune away excess facts. Include only those facts that are necessary to the legal problems to be resolved.

2. Avoid quotations of any kind—court decisions, testimony, statutes, documents—unless a brief reference or paraphrase is inadequate.

3. Don't belabour the obvious. Avoid multiple citations unless, for example, it is important to show a trend. Avoid explaining and supporting well-trodden legal principles. Avoid amplifying easy arguments. Avoid repetition.

4. Resist the temptation to pursue side-issues.

5. Revise with conciseness in mind, keeping your eye on the issues. Facts, quotations, arguments—the length of these units depends upon the issues of the case as a whole. The crucial question in revision is, what can I cut without sacrificing my argument?

Because the test for exclusion of materials is relevance to the issues, conciseness often comes about as an unintended by-product of conceptual revision. You are more likely to be concise if you have clearly framed the issues. One can achieve conciseness, in short, by not thinking about it at all, merely by keen attention to the logic of one's argument. Two of the exercises provided in Chapter 2 have, I hope, already made that point: the one on "Facts," and the one on "Structure." By focusing on organization, as the instructions required, you were probably able to save words as well. You might review those exercises at this point to see whether you have already applied the five suggestions above.

Since excessive quotations bedevil many judgments, and since the tendency to quote at length seems deeply embedded in legal practice, the third suggestion—"avoid quotations of any kind . . . unless a brief reference or paraphrase is inadequate"—requires some elaboration. What is the problem with quoting?

I have asked this question of many judges over the years in the following way: "As a reader, what do you do when you come to a long quotation in a judgment?" The most common answer is "skip it." On occasion, I hear, "skim until I find the italicized words and the statement 'italics added'." This is a promising area for psycholinguistic research. What is it about a mere indentation on a page that can make the eyes glaze over, the mind fidget, and the finger move restlessly to the next page? I suspect it is a conditioned reflex, a healthy Pavlovian response to habitual experience: if I read this, the mind thinks, I am bound to be bored and more likely to be confused than enlightened. Conciseness is not the only virtue sacrificed by quotation; clarity usually accompanies her to the altar.

Consider, for example, the following opening to a judgment:

The appellant, Charles Morgan, was charged with and convicted of a violation of the *Retail Business Holidays Act*, R.S.O. 1980, c. 453, and in particular s. 2(1), which reads as follows:

2.(1) Every person carrying on a retail business in a retail business establishment shall ensure that no member of the public is admitted thereto and no goods or services are sold or offered for sale therein by retail on a holiday.

In paragraph 1.(1) (a) of the Act, "holiday" is defined as follows:

1.(1) (a) "holiday" means:
  (i) New Year's Day,
  (ii) Good Friday,
  (iii) Victoria Day,
  (iv) Dominion Day
  (v) Labour Day,
  (vi) Thanksgiving Day
  (vii) Christmas Day
  (viii) Boxing Day
  (ix) Sunday, and
  (x) any other public holiday declared by proclamation of the Lieutenant Governor to be a holiday for the purposes of this Act;

Both at the trial and on appeal, the Courts were informed that the circumstances were not in dispute. . . .

Readers of the above introduction are bound to be confused. What is really at issue in the first quotation, we ask: whether the business was a *retail* business? whether the customer was a *member of the public*? whether the services were *sold* or *offered*? whether the date in question was a *holiday*? Any one of these questions might be important.

Once we arrive at the second quotation, we begin to suspect that the issue is whether the date in question was indeed a holiday. But we still cannot be sure. And since we assume that the texts quoted must be important (why else would they be quoted?), we continue to grope through them in an attempt to discover why.

The problem in this judgment, as you might have guessed already, is that the quotations are not important at all. As the argument unfolds, it becomes gradually clear that Charles Morgan did nothing more than sell a customer a shirt on Boxing Day. The meaning, the significance, the application of the *Retail Business Holidays Act* were not in dispute at all. For the purposes of the judgment, then, the opening could have been reduced to something like this:

37

The appellant, Charles Morgan, owner of Morgan Brothers, Clothiers, sold a shirt to a customer on Boxing Day in 1987. For this he was charged with and convicted of violating the *Retail Business Holidays Act*, R.S.O. 1980, c. 453, which prohibits the retail sale of goods on a holiday (2.1) and specifies Boxing Day as a holiday (1.1.a.viii).

The revision is not very elegant, but it is both clearer and more concise than the original. To decide this case, the judge had to read the full texts of the passages originally quoted; judicial altruism, however, requires that the judge not inflict the same pain upon the reader.

The temptations to quote are many, but the reasons for quoting are few. Since excessive quotation is a judicial habit, it must be consciously resisted. The question, as indicated in suggestion number two above, is when is a brief allusion or a paraphrase inadequate? Here are two answers:

1. When the meaning or significance of the document in question is in dispute.

2. When a paraphrase would achieve less clarity and conciseness than the original.

There may be other reasons for quoting, but the exceptions will not disprove the rules above. If you know that counsel for the defence does not have ready access to the authority you rely on for an argument, you might bend the rule and quote at length for that reason; you might achieve the same effect, however, at less cost to the elegance of your judicial style, by providing counsel with a separate photocopy of the authority in question.

Let's consider an example of the first rule, above: when the meaning or significance of the document in question is in dispute. You may recognize this example from the exercises on introductions. The original judgment upon which that exercise was based required consideration not only of the wording of a statute in English but in French:

Section 18(1)(1) of *Income Tax Act*, Stats. Can. 1970-71-72, c.63 provides that certain kinds of business expenses are not to be allowed as deductions in computing a taxpayer's taxable income:

In computing the income of a taxpayer from a business or property no deduction shall be made in respect of:

an outlay or expense made . . . for the use or maintenance of property that is a *yacht*, a camp, a lodge or a golf course . . .

(italics added)

The French version of the provision reads as follows:

Dans le calcul du revenu du contribuable, tiré d'une entreprise ou d'un bien, les éléments suivants ne sont pas déductibles:

un débours ou une dépense faite . . . pour l'usage ou l'entretien d'un bien qui est *un bateau de plaisance*, un pavillon, un chalet, un terrain de golf . . .

(italics added)

In the above case a judicial clear-cutter might argue that a paraphrase would suffice. Perhaps it would. What would be lost if we simply said that the *Income Tax Act* prevents business deductions for the hiring of yachts? Because the meaning of the word "yacht" is at issue, and because meaning is often determined by context, the inclusion of the brief quotation (notice that it is an *excerpt*) helps to clarify what is meant by a yacht: it is put into a class that includes such things as camps, lodges, and golf courses. Since this is a federal matter, moreover, the wording in French is also potentially important. The judge must ask whether the meaning or connotations of "*un bateau de plaisance*" are precisely the same as those for the word "yacht." In this situation, then, a *brief* quotation grounds the legal question: is this converted tugboat a yacht?

The second reason for quoting, when a paraphrase would achieve less clarity and conciseness than the original, can be illustrated by the following:

> The Respondent's application for a declaration to this effect was dismissed by the Motions Judge, who concluded that his statutory release date should be determined
>
>> by calculating two thirds of the time remaining, that is, starting from the date he was taken into custody and his parole suspended (May 14, 1989) and ending with the date of his sentence of imprisonment as originally imposed by the Court.   (p.6, A.B.p. 14)
>
> The Crown now appeals from that portion of the decision, arguing that the correct reference date should have been the date of revocation of his parole, not its suspension.

Although the wording of the Motions Judge is unlikely to be included in collections of elegant judicial style, it does the job, and it is hard to imagine a paraphrase doing it significantly better. Since the appeal is against the specific action embedded in the quotation, moreover, the setting of a statutory release date, the precise wording of the passage takes on additional significance.

In both of the above cases the quotations have been brief. The judges have selected the relevant words and enough of the context to clarify their meaning. They have not asked us to wade through a page of useless verbiage before arriving at the single phrase, with italics maddeningly added, at issue. They have resisted the easy temptation, in short, to cut and paste.

*   *   *

Exercises: Conciseness
Exercise Key, p. 96

1. *Review all of the exercises in Chapters 2 and 3 with conciseness in mind. Compare the length of your revisions with the length of the revisions in the Exercise Key. (Conciseness will also be at issue in the chapter on paragraphs and sentences).*

2. *Revise the following passage so that the quotations are either omitted or reduced in length. In doing so, you will probably increase the clarity of the passage and perhaps its grace.*

The applicants' main argument in this case is that given the serious nature of the allegations, of a plot to undertake certain actions in the future, a greater amount of information should be disclosed about the informant(s) against them than might be disclosed in another type of case. Given the nature of the allegations, there is no concrete evidence available to either support or refute the allegations; thus the applicants state that additional information, for example, concerning the informant(s) must be disclosed. Otherwise, it is argued, the applicants can be the victims of any inmate who concocts a credible sounding story.

What is particularly troubling about the facts in this case is the nature of the affidavit evidence which has been filed. Stuart Reese, an employee of Correctional Service Canada, filed an affidavit with respect to the information which had been disclosed to the applicants when they made their request. The affidavit states as follows:

> 7. Now produced and shown to me and marked as Exhibit "C" to this my affidavit are the contents of the security file regarding the transfer of William Leland Black, F.P.S. 74568Y, and Brewster Thiessen, F.P.S. 665783W, from Pratt Institution to Alberta Penitentiary, Special Treatment Unit, which transfer gives rise to this litigation; save and except, those documents which by their disclosure could reveal the identity of confidential informants.

> 8. Documents which, by their disclosure could reveal the identity of confidential informants, have been summarized in the document attached hereto as a part of Exhibit "C" entitled "Security Information."

Mr. Justice Kilroy in speaking for the Federal Court of Appeal in *Marco v. Regional Transfer Board and Smith*, (1992) 2 F.C. 37 at 66-67, wrote:

> The burden is always on the authorities to demonstrate that they have withheld only such information as is strictly necessary for the purpose of protecting the safety of the informer. . . . In the final analysis, the test must be not whether there exist good grounds for withholding information but

rather whether enough information has been revealed to allow the person concerned to answer the case against him.

The *Corrections and Conditional Release Act*, S.C. 1992, c. 20 provides:

27.(1) Where an offender is entitled by this Part or the regulations to make representations in relation to a decision to be taken by the Service about the offender, the person or body that is to take the decision shall, subject to subsection (3), give the offender, a reasonable period before the decision is to be taken, all the information to be considered in the taking of the decision or a summary of that information.

. . .

27.(3) . . . where the Commissioner has reasonable grounds to believe that disclosure of information under subsection (1) or (2) would jeopardize

(a) the safety of any person,
(b) the security of a penitentiary, or
(c) the conduct of any lawful investigation,

the Commissioner may authorize the withholding from the offender of as much information as is strictly necessary in order to protect the interest identified in paragraph (a), (b), or (c).

The affidavit filed does not purport to have applied these criteria when reviewing whether or not additional information could have been provided to the applicants.

CHAPTER 4

Paragraphs and Sentences

"Why, sir, for my part, I say the gentleman had drunk
himself out of his five sentences"
Merry Wives of Windsor, 1.1.174-75

As a beginning teacher of first-year composition, I once had a student come up to me at the end of class and ask, earnestly, "How long is a paragraph?"

As the following quotation shows, effective paragraphs can be at least as long as six sentences and as short as a single sentence:

> We turn then to the contention that the necessary connection between the government and the policy and contracts here in issue is established by the fact that the university is exercising a delegated governmental function. We assume, for the purposes of this argument, that a subordinate body carrying out a public function on behalf of government, may, in carrying out that function, be bound by the Charter. This is consistent with the purpose of the Charter, namely, to protect individual rights against the undue encroachment of the more powerful state. We also assume that it can be said that the government has delegated to the university the task of providing post-secondary education to the public. The question then is whether that delegation establishes a direct and precisely defined connection between the government and the university's policy of mandatory retirement and the contracts embodying it. Can that policy be regarded as an exercise of government power?

> In our opinion, the answer to these questions is no.

Both the clarity and drama of the final sentence would have been undermined if it had closed off the preceding paragraph.

Judges tend to write shorter paragraphs than academics. This is not because academics are more long-winded, although such may be the case, but because they are more likely to spend most of their words developing ideas. Sections of judgments dealing with legal argument, therefore, are likely to have relatively long paragraphs. Sections dealing with facts or procedures or documentation are likely to have short paragraphs because they do not require development.

Although it is impossible to define a right length for a paragraph, it is possible to experience wrong lengths. Paragraphs can induce vertigo in readers in two opposed ways: by never ending or by ending too soon too often. If a five-page paragraph is likely to confuse a reader, imagine the effect of five pages of single-sentence paragraphs. The one makes the reader yearn for divisions, the other, for unifications. The reason for such frustration, in both cases, is simple: readers need their meaning in bite-sized pieces, not a single pea or an entire cutlet at a time.

A paragraph, then, is a signal for a developed idea. Usually, but not always, a paragraph is longer than a sentence. This means that the thought within a paragraph must be unified, must cohere internally. But it also means that a paragraph must be joined effectively to the one that precedes and the one that follows it; it must enable transitions. First-year composition handbooks often advise students to introduce each paragraph with a sentence that both provides a transition to the preceding paragraph and establishes the topic of the one at hand, and to end each paragraph with a sentence that prepares for the next. Here is an example of that method:

> It may be suggested that the introduction of a defence based on due diligence and the shifting of the burden of proof might better be implemented by legislative act. In answer, it should be recalled that the concept of absolute liability and the creation of a jural category of public welfare offences are both the product of the judiciary and not of the Legislature. The development to date of this defence, in the numerous decisions I have referred to, of Courts in this country as well as in Australia and New Zealand, has also been the work of Judges. The present case offers the opportunity of consolidating and clarifying the doctrine.
>
> The correct approach . . .

The first sentence of the full paragraph above looks backward towards arguments already made about due diligence and the burden of proof; it looks forward to the topic at hand—why not depend upon legislative act rather than the judiciary to implement this defence? The final sentence of the paragraph hints at what is to follow: the "correct approach," which is to "consolidate" and "clarify" the doctrine in a particular way.

Not all paragraphs will be so methodical. Consider, for example, the paragraphs quoted previously to illustrate differences in length. The opening sentence of the first paragraph begins with a strong transitional signal— "We turn then to the contention"—and then continues with the topic at hand: whether the "university is exercising a delegated governmental function." The paragraph concludes with its transitional signal delivered in the form of a question: "Can that policy be regarded as an exercise of government power?" I suspect that most readers do not anticipate an immediate reply to that question; it is not common for a judgment to put the conclusion before the arguments. For this reason, we probably do not take that question as preparation for the next paragraph. When it comes, then, the answer is a surprise: we have been prepared for an answer, but not for one so soon. Now that we have the answer, moreover, we have the entire topic of the paragraph. But we lack an explicit transitional signal to the next. Or do we? A transitional signal of a general kind, at least, is embedded in the answer: the reasons for the negative must now be explained. Although it might seem an exception to the handbook approach, in short, this example is actually a subtle variation upon it.

The value of transitional signals and topic sentences becomes especially clear in the case of quotations, which often appear without them. How often have you read passages in judgments that proceed like the following?

> In *Mills v. The Queen* (1986) 26 CCC (3d) 481 (S.C.C.) at 538-9 Lamer J. stated:
>
>> Additionally, under s.11(b), the security of the person is to be safe-guarded as jealously as the liberty of the individual. In this context, the concept of security of the person is not restricted to physical integrity; rather, it encompasses protection against 'overlong subjection to the vexations and vicissitudes of a pending criminal accusation' . . . These include stigmatization of the accused, loss of privacy, stress and anxiety resulting from a multitude of factors, including possible disruption of family, social life and work, legal costs, uncertainty as to the outcome and sanction. These forms of prejudice cannot be disregarded nor mini-mized when assessing the reasonableness of the delay.
>>
>> In my view there is an inference of prejudice due to the delay in pro-cessing this matter. The applicant's testimony includes many references to the severe effects this delay has had upon his wife and children and his ability to sustain a proper home environment.

The opening sentence in the above example provides neither a transition from the preceding paragraph nor a topic for the paragraph at hand; it merely tells us that Lamer J. said something in 1986. Once we have read the quotation, moreover, we are not prepared for the inference of preju-dice that ensues; the discontinuity between the quotation and the conclu-sion apparently drawn from it is re-enforced by the fact that they are separated by being parts of two different paragraphs.

These problems might be solved, or at least mitigated, by a revision like the following:

> In *Mills v. The Queen* (1986) Lamer J. held that reasonableness of delay must be tested against the security of the person, a concept that includes but goes beyond physical integrity:
>
>> Additionally, under s.11(b), the security of the person is to be safe-guarded as jealously as the liberty of the individual. In this context, the

concept of security of the person is not restricted to physical integrity; rather, it encompasses protection against 'overlong subjection to the vexations and vicissitudes of a pending criminal accusation' . . . These include stigmatization of the accused, loss of privacy, stress and anxiety resulting from a multitude of factors, including possible disruption of family, social life and work, legal costs, uncertainty as to the outcome and sanction. These forms of prejudice cannot be disregarded nor minimized when assessing the reasonableness of the delay.

(*Mills v. The Queen* (1986), 26 CCC (3d) 481 (S.C.C.) at 538-9)

Since the applicant's testimony makes clear that the delay has had a severely negative effect upon his family life, one must infer that the security of his person has been impaired and the delay has been prejudicial.

The above revision begins with a topic sentence and concludes with an inference drawn from the quotation; unlike the original, it allows the reader to trace the *development* of the idea in question. Since they are often parts of an argument, quotations often need such treatment; before the quotation, the reader should be told what is coming, and after, what it signifies. Lay readers, in particular, need this assistance, for their minds do not run on the well polished rails of legal argument.

In the above example, I have kept the original quotation intact. The surgically inclined might want to revise still further and produce something like this:

In *Mills v. The Queen* (1986) Lamer J. held that reasonableness of delay must be tested against the security of the person, a concept that includes such factors as the disruption of family life attendant upon pending criminal accusation; see 26 CCC (3d) 481 (S.C.C.) at 538-9. Since the applicant's testimony makes clear that the delay has had a severely negative effect upon his family life, one must conclude that the security of his person has been impaired and the delay has been prejudicial.

Although this version omits the full explanatory context provided by the original quotation, it highlights the organization of the paragraph as a whole. In so doing it reminds us that quotations are parts of paragraphs and must be treated accordingly.

To sum up:

1. A paragraph is as long as it needs to be.
2. Long paragraphs can induce vertigo, as can an extended number of one-sentence paragraphs.
3. An effective argumentative paragraph usually includes a topic sentence, a conclusion, and transitions at both ends.
4. Quotations should be treated as parts of paragraphs.

*   *   *

Exercises: Paragraphs and Sentences
Exercise Key, p. 97

Revise the following, with specific attention to effective paragraphing:

1. On Mondays the girls return to their mother after school, and she cares for them for the rest of the day.

    On Tuesdays they both spend the day in school, but Jane goes to their mother for the afternoon and evening, while Rebecca goes to their father until 9:00 p.m., when she returns to their mother.

    On Wednesdays after school both girls go to their father, who keeps them overnight and delivers them to school the next morning.

    On Thursdays after school Rebecca returns to her mother, while Jane goes to her father, returning to her mother at 9:00 p.m.

    On Fridays after school both girls go to their maternal grandparents, who keep them until Saturday at noon.

    The girls return to their mother on Saturday afternoon and remain with her throughout Sunday.

2. I am not convinced, on the evidence available to me, that Ms. Cotton's failure to address this matter in her affidavit means that her motivation is even partly dependent on a desire to frustrate access between Joseph and Mr. Rivers. Prior to the end of 1989, Ms. Cotton had not permitted Joseph to stay overnight with Mr. Rivers, although he was frequently in Mr. Rivers' care during the day. Ms. Cotton swears in her affidavit that she did not permit overnight access because of certain sexual practices on the part of Mr. Rivers. She does not specify the nature of these sexual acts. I am, therefore, unable to attach any weight to this statement as I cannot assess the reasonableness of her conclusion. In any event, Ms. Cotton has lived with Mr. Rivers on more than one occasion and has permitted overnight access since late 1989. Mr. Rivers has always been fairly involved in Joseph's day to day life despite the fact that he has resided with Joseph (and his mother) for only about 19 months in total and has been having overnight access for only about 6 months. I have assumed in calculating the 19 month figure that the fifth line in paragraph 6 of Ms. Cotton's affidavit should read 'winter of 1987' rather than 'winter of 1996'. I do not attach any weight to Ms. Cotton's statement in her affidavit that in the past Mr. Rivers did not see his son on weekends. He was spending a lot of time with Joseph during the week and if he did not see Joseph during the weekends, then Ms. Cotton was able to do so during her weekends off.

* * *

Sentences

Sentences, like paragraphs, should be as long as they need to be. Addicts of plain English often advise writers to keep their sentences short. The advice makes some sense. Long sentences are more likely to cause trouble than short ones. But to apply a formula of this kind is to risk absurdity. All short sentences are not good sentences, and all long ones not bad. The point is not to write short sentences but effective ones.

Sentences may go wrong in many ways: through faulty punctuation, flabbiness in verbs, wordiness, structural imbalance, poor word choice, and other infelicities without number. Before we explore the minefields, however, let's take a moment to admire a garden. Here are three wonderful sentences:

> Vigorous writing is concise. A sentence should contain no unnecessary words, a paragraph no unnecessary sentences, for the same reason that a drawing should have no unnecessary lines and a machine no unnecessary parts. This requires not that the writer make all his sentences short, or that he avoid all detail and treat his subjects only in outline, but that every word tell.

The author of these immortal lines is William Strunk, Jr., and the book is *The Elements of Style* (see the Reading List).

Why are these sentences impressive? To be concise, I'll list only seven reasons (in no particular order):

1. The punctuation re-enforces both the meaning and the rhythm of the sentences.
2. With the exception of the first sentence, the verbs are active and forceful. Two achieve dramatic effect by departing slightly from normal usage: "requires not" rather than "does not require," and "tell" rather than "count" or "fulfill its exact function."
3. Every word tells. The passage enacts its meaning.
4. The diction is simple.
5. The metaphors both focus and expand the meaning.
6. The long sentences are tightly structured through parallelism. For example:
   A sentence should contain no unnecessary words
   a paragraph no unnecessary sentences
   . . .
   a drawing should have no unnecessary lines
   a machine no unnecessary parts.
7. The variety of the sentences gives form to the paragraph. The topic sentence, for example, is short; the concluding sentence achieves climax with the unexpected brevity of "that every word tell."

47

If Strunk can wring poetry out of the rules of composition, then perhaps even the law can be wrestled into prose.

The most common sentence problems in judgments can be grouped under three headings: punctuation, word choice, and structure. Let's examine each one in order.

Punctuation

Judges often find the rules of punctuation as mystifying as English professors find the rules of law. Any attempt to impose a system upon the vagaries of human experience ultimately fails, of course, and the rules for the comma are no less imperfect than those of the *Criminal Code*. But for all its imperfections, the legal system functions, as do the rules of punctuation. In most cases, indeed, the rules function quite well. What follows are not the complicated (and truly interesting) rules of punctuation, but the commonplace, the routine.

One of the chief problems, or, more optimistically, challenges in punctuating is the variety of choices available. Sometimes a comma is needed for logic. Suppose, for example, a park contains a single monument, a huge stone sculpture that is at the point of collapse. We might report the destruction of the monument as follows:

He destroyed the monument, which had been declared unsafe.

In this sentence the comma is necessary to the meaning. With the comma, the sentence tells us that there is only one monument at issue and that it has been destroyed. Without the comma, the sentence would tell us that more than one monument is at issue, and that only one, the one declared unsafe, has been destroyed:

He destroyed the monument which had been declared unsafe.

Depending upon our meaning, in short, we will choose to include or exclude the comma.

Sometimes, however, commas serve only a rhetorical effect, usually to create a pause. Some writers, for example (not me), would add no punctuation to the following sentence:

Here for example is the way to measure concrete.

Some, however, would add commas:

Here, for example, is the way to measure concrete.

The former sentence has the virtue of speed; the latter, of a measured pace. I prefer the latter and, for reasons that will shortly become clear, I recommend the latter to judges.

48

To appreciate the range of available choices, it might help to consider two distinctive styles of punctuation—styles that we might label informal and formal. Let's review the same sentence done in different ways. Here is the informal version:

> In the loveliest town of all, where the houses were white and high and the elm trees were green and higher than the houses, where the front yards were wide and pleasant and the back yards were bushy and worth finding out about, where the streets sloped down to the stream and the stream flowed quietly under the bridge, where the lawns ended in orchards and the orchards ended in fields and the fields ended in pastures and the pastures climbed the hill and disappeared over the top toward the wonderful wide sky, in this loveliest of all towns Stuart stopped to get a drink of sarsaparilla.

Here is the formal version:

> In the loveliest town of all, where the houses were white and high, and the elm trees were green and higher than the houses; where the front yards were wide and pleasant, and the back yards were bushy and worth finding out about; where the streets sloped down to the stream, and the stream flowed quietly under the bridge; where the lawns ended in orchards, and the orchards ended in fields, and the fields ended in pastures, and the pastures climbed the hill and disappeared over the top toward the wonderful wide sky: in this loveliest of all towns Stuart stopped to get a drink of sarsaparilla.

The author is E. B. White, the novel is *Stuart Little*, and the original punctuation, as I hope you guessed, is informal. Both versions can be justified on technical grounds. But the informal version is infinitely superior in evoking the breathless wonder of childhood experience. The formal version clogs the meandering pathway with unnecessary and distracting directional signals.

Sometimes directional signals are extremely useful. Readers tend to need them, for example, in judgments; hence my recommendation that judges adopt a relatively formal mode of punctuation. In practice, this means more commas, more semicolons, more colons, and fewer dashes and parentheses. Let's consider the essential rules of punctuation with judgment writing in mind.

Comma

1. Commas precede the coordinating conjunctions *and, but, nor, for, or* and the connectives *so* and *yet* between main clauses.

    EXAMPLE: In such a case, government power would be exercised, and it is that government power which attracts Charter scrutiny.

COMMENT: *Notice that the rule specifies* main *clauses: clauses that could stand alone as sentences. If the clauses are short, the comma is discretionary and usually omitted by informal punctuators.*

2. Commas follow introductory elements such as adverb clauses, long phrases, transitional expressions, and interjections.

   EXAMPLE: Although the provincial government has the power to appoint and dismiss a majority of the members of the board of governors, its power to dominate the board is removed by the statutory provision that two of the eight members must be nominated by the Alumni Association.

   COMMENT: *If the introductory element is short and closely related to the main clause, informal punctuators sometimes omit it.*

3. Commas separate items in a series.

   EXAMPLE: Age-based distinctions can be found in *The Young Offenders Act*, the *Age of Majority Act*, the *Infants Act*, and the *Liquor Control Act*.

   COMMENT: *Many of us learned from our grade eight teachers—why were they all so terrifying?—that the final comma before the conjunction was to be omitted on pain of instant expulsion. Informal punctuators take this lesson to heart. Formal punctuators, however, preferring to be safe than sorry, include the comma because its omission will occasionally create ambiguity, as in the following example:*

   The statutes concerning environmental protection, worker's compensation, public health and safety were passed by the legislature.

   How many statutes were passed by the legislature, three or four?

4. Commas set off nonrestrictive clauses and phrases and other parenthetical elements.

   EXAMPLE: We conclude that, in the abstract, these objectives might be considered capable of overriding a right guaranteed by the *Charter*.

   COMMENT: *Make sure you include* both *commas for parenthetical elements; they serve as brackets, isolating interruptions, so that the true path of the sentence remains clear.*

   EXAMPLE: We oppose an increase in taxes, which would be inflationary.

   COMMENT: *Notice that the meaning changes if this comma is omitted. If we include the comma, we oppose* any *increase in taxes; all increases are inflationary by definition. If we exclude the comma, we oppose only tax increases that would be inflationary; non-inflationary tax increases are acceptable. Be-*

cause of this potential ambiguity, many writers prefer to avoid the use of the word "which" in such cases, preferring "that." If we write "We oppose any increases in taxes that would be inflationary," only one meaning is possible: we oppose only increases that would be inflationary but can accept increases that are not inflationary.

Semicolon

1. Use a semicolon between two main clauses not linked by a coordinating conjunction (*and, but, or, nor, for*) or by the connectives *so* and *yet*.

    EXAMPLE: In such a case, government power would be exercised; it is that government power which attracts Charter scrutiny.

    EXAMPLE: The criminal asked for mercy; however, his victim demanded justice.

    COMMENT: *In all cases under this rule a semicolon may be replaced by a period. Since this is so, why use semicolons? For one reason only: the semicolon signals a close logical relationship between the two parts of the sentence. To use a semicolon, then, is to emphasize logical continuity; to use a period is to suggest separation. For this reason sentences that aspire towards tight syntactical symmetry, like the one immediately preceding, usually take semicolons.*

2. Use a semicolon to separate a series of items which themselves contain commas.

    EXAMPLE: The following were called as witnesses: John Smith, a bricklayer; Sarah Miles, a nurse at Royal Jubilee Hospital; George Jenkins, an ambulance driver; and Rebecca Walsh, an accountant.

    COMMENT: *Notice how confusing the above sentence would be if we relied solely on commas.*

Colon

1. Use a colon to direct attention to an explanation or summary, a series, or a quotation.

    EXAMPLE: The appellant raises three issues: first, whether the arbitrator erred in concluding that the College was government within section 32 of the Charter; second, whether the collective agreement was law; and third, whether the arbitrator was competent to determine those issues.

    EXAMPLE: He did what was called for in the circumstances: he ran.

    COMMENT: *My grade eight teacher told me that a colon was simply another way of saying "that is." A useful tip.*

Parentheses

1. Use parentheses (sometimes called round brackets) to enclose incidental remarks.

   EXAMPLE: See the sentence above.

   EXAMPLE: The respondent, Seabreeze Ltd. (Seabreeze), claims that the property in question was not suitable for a ski resort.

   COMMENT: *Parentheses should be used sparingly in judgments. They are useful for incidental information, as exemplified. Used too often, however, they create the Molly Bloom effect of stream-of-consciousness. If a remark is truly incidental, perhaps it doesn't belong at all.*

Dash

1. Use the dash for sharp interruptions, additions, or illustrations.

   EXAMPLE: Such delays in the course of justice cannot—and must not—be tolerated.

   EXAMPLE: The common notion that lawyers cannot write plain English has now been exposed for what it is—an illusion.

   COMMENT: *Dashes should be used sparingly in judgments. They often carry a high emotional charge and, since they perform many of the tasks of other punctuation marks, such as the comma, colon, and parentheses, their use can become addictive. Beginning novelists, who often couple strong imaginations with weak punctuation, sometimes get high on the dash, with breathtaking results.*

*   *   *

Exercises: Punctuation
Exercise Key, p. 98

Add the correct punctuation to the following sentences. Since the sentences have been taken from actual judgments, they are not invariably elegant. Resist the temptation to do more than add punctuation.

1. Lastly in this discourse on "fundamental justice" I wish to mention that the social and historical context in which this question is viewed should not be limited to common law or pre-*Charter* history.

2. Dr. John R. Lawson Director of the Department of Legal Affairs said that in spite of the allegations his Department would continue its present policy.

3. At this early stage in the development of the *Charter* the principles of fundamental justice have not been fully explored.

4. Earlier last year probably in response to the Commission's inquiry the House of Commons sitting in special session enacted the recommended legislation.

5. In my opinion the primary test should be a practical one based on the only valid justification for the rule against duplicity does the accused know the case he has to meet or is he prejudiced in the preparation of his defence by ambiguity in the charge?

6. In this doctrine it is not up to the prosecution to prove negligence instead it is open to the defendant to prove that all due care has been taken.

7. The present case concerns the interpretation of two troublesome words frequently found in public welfare statutes "cause" and "effect."

8. A homeowner who pays a fee for the collection of his garbage by a business which services the area could probably not be said to have caused or permitted the pollution if the collector dumps the garbage in the river.

9. In this case the father has demonstrated his ability to provide for his son's material welfare but he has not demonstrated his ability to provide a supportive home environment.

10. The applicants seek to quash those decisions on the grounds that they were denied a fair hearing that they were not given enough information concerning the reasons for the transfer in order to be able to respond to those reasons adequately that their submissions were not considered in any meaningful way by the Deputy Commissioner and that the decisions were biased.

11. It is trite law that safeguards that pertain to prosecution for a criminal offence do not pertain to prison management decisions the Warden for example did not need to be satisfied beyond a reasonable doubt that the plot existed.

12. On the date in question her counsel presented three witnesses Dr. George Sims a surgeon who has known the defendant for fourteen years Michael Walsh an addictions counsellor at the Summerville Treat-

ment Centre who treated the defendant for six months and Heather Wong who has been a friend of the defendant's family for many years.

13. Fear of punishment then is but one factor to be considered in evaluating sincerity.

14. The regulations were not followed in this case and the applicant's grievance was dealt with by the Commissioner at an inappropriate time.

15. In some situations even though bias or a reasonable apprehension of bias may be said to exist a decision will still be upheld on the grounds of necessity.

16. In deciding which of these two options is in Lester's best interests I must weigh the enumerated criteria found in sections 65(1) and 37(3) of the *Child and Family Services Act* (C.F.C.A.) keeping in mind the principles that govern these sections.

17. Parliament has not mandated a minimum term of imprisonment but has left the appropriate penalty to the discretion of the trial court.

18. At the site the police found the following weapons two shotguns one revolver three hunting knives and a .22 calibre rifle.

19. Mr. Jones is an alcoholic the evidence is clear in that regard.

20. Disrupting Carol's sleep at night failing to provide her with adequate meals arguing violently in her presence these are not actions that recommend continued custody.

*   *   *

Wordiness

"Vigorous writing," say Strunk and White, "is concise." Most judgments are afflicted with wordiness, not because their authors are unusually loquacious but because they do not revise. Stream-of-consciousness sentences are more likely to carry along flotsam and jetsam than argosies laden with meaning. In oral judgments, much wordiness occurs because the judge is literally thinking aloud, depending upon stock phrases to fill in gaps in the same way that Homeric bards depended upon traditional epithets. All first drafts are wordy; pruning is by definition an exercise in revision.

Let's consider a typical instance of wordiness:

The fact that his plans for the three of them as a family did not materialize is not a basis on which he can now revoke his established parental relationship to the child (*Re Murphy and Chambers*, unreported decision of Mercer, A.C.J., December 20, 1983) and thereby withdraw from his support obligations.

Since conciseness comes from revision, it might be helpful to ask how we might attack such a sentence if it appeared in one of our own first drafts. How does one locate wordiness and how does one root it out? Often, one can tell at a glance—the sheer length of the sentence engenders suspicion. Often, too, the mind will begin to cloud over as one reads. If one reads aloud, a faltering voice will often reveal when meaning gets lost in thickets of verbiage.

When I have located a suspicious sentence, I find it helpful to zero in on the words that seem to carry the meaning. In this case, I would underline "plans," "three," "not materialize," "revoke," "parental relationship," "withdraw," and "support obligations." Then I would ask whether the sentence can be divided; in most cases, division is the simplest way to clarify such sentences. Can we divide this sentence and prune away the clutter that obscures its central ideas? Here is one attempt:

His parental relationship to the child is established in *Murphy and Chambers* (unreported decision of Mercer, A.C.J., December 20, 1983). The failure of his plans for the three of them cannot justify revoking this relationship and the support obligation it imposes.

Here is another, in a single sentence:

The failure of his plans for the three of them cannot justify revoking the parental relationship and consequent support obligation established in *Murphy and Chambers* (unreported decision of Mercer, A.C.J., December 20, 1983).

The revisions are not very elegant, but then neither is the original. The first revision at least saves eleven words, or twenty percent; the second revision saves nineteen words, or thirty-five percent. More importantly, both revisions gain in clarity.

Wordiness, then, often appears in two guises: as sentences that need dividing, and as extraneous words or phrases. Certain phrases are dangerous offenders. Here is a brief list that might be personalized with your own favourite additions and framed above a desk:

The fact that . . .
This is a situation in which . . .

For a period of . . .
There is no doubt that . . .
It is his belief that . . .

Notice how often the word "that" appears in such constructions. There is no doubt that it is worth a careful look when revising (if you didn't notice the wordiness in this sentence, re-read the entire section).

Some wordiness is specific to legal writing. Consider, for example, the following:

last will and testament
cease and desist
force and effect
free and clear

These doublets, we are told by legal scholars, derive from the time when English lawyers had two languages to choose from and wanted to touch both bases. Whatever their original use, they are now no more than ritual incantations, a ready source for spoofs of lawyers in situation comedies.

* * *

Exercises: Wordiness
Exercise Key, p. 101

Reduce the length of the following sentences without changing their meaning. You should notice that clarity increases as length decreases.

1. It is at this juncture that the facts become somewhat murky.

2. It was the conclusion of the Hydro workers at trial that, based on a burn mark on the primary power line and another on the backhoe, that the Appellants themselves had caused the power outage.

3. All of this is not to suggest that large quantities of this material, namely "activated sludge" could not present harm or adversely impact upon the river.

4. The Crown advises this Court that the tape has in fact been lost.

5. Accordingly, I am of the view that a de facto assessment of the relationship of the accused and the complainants is the appropriate one, and on that basis there is evidence sufficient to warrant a committal on each of the s. 153 charges.

6. It is the fact that the father canceled so many of his weekends with Sarah that has led to the mother bringing this application.

7. In this situation I am of the opinion that the evidence that Mr. Harris has given is somewhat inconclusive.

8. The membership contract of the country club provided that in the event that Mr. Mesky missed more than two consecutive payments all privileges would be revoked by the country club.

9. One thing that must be considered in this case is whether or not the best interests of Giles are served by his being supervised by his grandparents on a regular basis.

10. But when I have evidence of the description offered by the arresting officer as merely a misdescription and that there was no other possibility except that it is and was an approved instrument that he used, I find that both the subjective and objective tests as set out in *Regina v. Storrey* have been met.

*   *   *

Sentence Structure

Many of the sentences above are not only wordy but ill-structured. The two faults are close companions. Structure not only produces clarity; it is a powerful tool for heightening meaning and rhetorical effect. Although the more oratorical kinds of structure are usually inappropriate to judgments, even oral judgments, awareness of these options might increase your stylistic versatility.

In Shakespeare's day bitter verbal wars were fought over the shape of sentences. One popular structure was modeled after Cicero and went by the name of Ciceronean. It was characterized by length, elaborate symmetries, and the suspension of meaning until the end. Here is Francis Bacon marveling in Ciceronean style at the learning of King James I. This kind of sentence builds towards a climactic effect:

> For it seemeth much in a King, if, by the compendious extractions of other men's wits and labours, he can take hold of any superficial ornaments and shows of learning; or if he countenance and prefer learning and learned men: but to drink indeed of the true fountains of learning, nay, to have such a fountain of learning in himself, in a King, and in a King born, is almost a miracle.

Bacon's own comments on prose style make clear that he valued such sentences only for their persuasive power; it is no coincidence that this example is taken from his preface to *The Advancement of Learning*, a work that he hoped would incite the King to establish a research institute to advance the new science.

In his *Essays* Bacon prefers another kind of sentence structure, generally called the Senecan. This kind of structure features brevity and tight symmetry. The *Essays* were intended not to persuade but to provoke thought. Here are a few examples:

> The stage is more beholding to love than the life of a man.

> He that hath wife and children hath given hostages to fortune.

> Some books are to be tasted, others to be swallowed, and some few to be chewed and digested.

Bacon heightens the effect of his terse symmetrical structures by vivid and precise metaphors.

The originator of the essay form, Michel de Montaigne, popularized what came to be known as the "loose" style, a style that establishes symmetries initially but then explodes them, creating something of the effect of Joyce's stream-of-consciousness. Here is a modern translation of one of Montaigne's sentences:

> Those who in my time have tried to correct the world's morals by new ideas, reform the superficial vices; the essential ones they leave as they were, if they do not increase them; and increase is to be feared.

While not exactly stream-of-consciousness, this kind of structure proceeds by unexpected turns, one thought breeding the next.

The shape of an effective sentence, then, depends in part upon the effect you are trying to achieve. To pursue these ideas would take us beyond mere questions of sentence structure and into judicial style, the subject of Chapter 6. In that chapter, I will suggest that judges have a range of different styles available, a range of structural effects. For the moment, let's concentrate on two important structural devices that are often misused in judgments. First, placement for emphasis, then parallelism.

Placement for emphasis

As the sentence you are reading illustrates, the emphatic position in a sentence, especially one that leads its reader through so many subordinate clauses and phrases that the meaning seems to recede farther and farther into the distance until it becomes a remote speck on the horizon, invisible to all but the most farsighted, is usually the end. Let's test this idea with a simple sentence:

58

These allegations were not supported by any proper evidence or particulars and basically were evidence of bad reputation.

Imprisoned in this miasmal sentence is an idea struggling to be released. How can we liberate it? Where should the emphasis be? Or, since it is hard to say from the original, where might it be? Suppose we allow the ending its emphatic role. We might try this:

These unsupported allegations show nothing more than a bad reputation.

In this version emphasis falls, first, on "bad reputation," second, on "unsupported allegations," and, third, on "show nothing more than." The sentence supports, in other words, the rhetoricians' customary claim that the most emphatic position in a sentence is the end, the second most emphatic the beginning.

Slipshod writers, or those confused about their priorities, ignore emphasis. The merely careless often try to achieve it in questionable ways:

These allegations show nothing more than a *bad reputation* and are unsupported by proper evidence.

Here the use of italics creates civil war within the sentence, with "*bad reputation*" and "proper evidence" struggling against each other for the reader's attention. Even when used appropriately, devices such as italics or repetition should be used sparingly in judgment writing; they call attention to themselves, creating a stridency of tone that is likely to unnerve a reader.

If we want the emphasis to fall on reputation, we should put the idea at the end. If we want the emphasis to fall on evidence, we should change the structure and put that idea at the end:

These allegations show nothing more than a bad reputation; they are unsupported by proper evidence.

Or:

These allegations, which show nothing more than a bad reputation, are unsupported by proper evidence.

In judgment writing, attention to placement is important not for emotional effect, as it might be in novels or sermons, but for clarity. And clarity benefits not only the reader. When the writer pauses to think about the creation of emphasis by positioning ideas within a sentence, the writer is forced to think hard about which idea is most important. The question forces clear thinking.

Parallelism

Here is an example of a sentence that needs re-structuring:

> At the Sentencing Hearing in this matter, the Subcommittee was provided with a copy of Mr. Fisher's Discipline Record, which reveals one complaint in 1984 resulting in the issuance of a caution and the requirement of an apology; four complaints during the years 1991 to 1993 that led to his being cautioned and counselled, and in 1992 there was a complaint resulting in the issuing of a reprimand arising from a complaint of delay and inactivity and non-response to the New Brunswick Barristers' Society.

Although this sentence is wordy, the dizziness it evokes results more from structural awkwardness than wordiness. In order for such a sentence to be clear, its structure must support its meaning. A careful look at the sentence reveals two main problems: the false signal of the semicolon after "apology," and the shift in structure marked by "in 1992 there was." In addition, the length of the sentence suggests that a break after "Record" in line two would ease comprehension.

Let's test several different ways of revising this sentence. Here is one version, which removes the semicolon and creates a parallel structure for each of the dependent clauses:

> At the Sentencing Hearing in this matter, the Subcommittee was provided with a copy of Mr. Fisher's Discipline Record, which reveals one complaint in 1984 resulting in a caution and the requirement of an apology, four complaints during the years 1991 to 1993 resulting in a caution and the requirement of counselling, and one complaint in 1992 resulting in a reprimand for delay, inactivity, and non-response to the New Brunswick Barristers' Society.

To achieve greater clarity, we can divide the sentence and prepare the reader for the onset of a list:

> At the Sentencing Hearing in this matter, the Subcommittee was provided with a copy of Mr. Fisher's Discipline Record. It reveals six complaints: one in 1984 resulting in a caution and the requirement of an apology; four during the years 1991 to 1993 resulting in a caution and the requirement of counselling; and one in 1992 resulting in a reprimand for delay, inactivity, and non-response to the New Brunswick Barristers' Society.

Although not required, the conversion of commas into semicolons enforces a separation between clauses that enhances clarity.

Although much improved, this sentence is still not quite right. What is wrong? The rhetoricians tell us that the conclusion of a sentence is the most emphatic position. The conclusion of this sentence consists of the following: "for delay, inactivity, and non-response to the New Brunswick Barristers' Society." Should that information receive emphasis? No. The preceding parts of the sentence focus on the general complaints and actions, not the particulars. So the meaning of the sentence goes awry at the end. The only way to solve that problem is to leave out the added information:

> At the Sentencing Hearing in this matter, the Subcommittee was provided with a copy of Mr. Fisher's Discipline Record. It reveals six complaints: one in 1984 resulting in a caution and the requirement of an apology; four during the years 1991 to 1993 resulting in a caution and the requirement of counselling; and one in 1992 resulting in a reprimand.

If the deleted information is important, it can be provided in a sentence of its own.

And then, for the truly fussy, a final version:

> At the Sentencing Hearing, the Subcommittee was provided with a copy of Mr. Fisher's Discipline Record, which reveals six complaints over nine years: one in 1984 resulting in a caution and a required apology; four during the years 1991 to 1993 resulting in a caution and required counselling; and one in 1992 resulting in a reprimand.

In this version I have highlighted a point that the original sentence obscures: the nine-year period in which the offenses occur. You will not be surprised to learn that this version reduces the length of the original by thirty-five percent. By focusing on structure, we achieve conciseness.

The moral to this rather long story (only an English professor could so anatomize a dead sentence) is simple: use parallel structures for parallel ideas. The form of a sentence, in short, should follow upon the content. Once you establish a structure, keep with it. Not:

> Ms. Borsky claims that Lois receives lunch money from her everyday, that she takes Lois to school in the morning, picking her up again in the afternoon, and Lois's homework is supervised by her every evening.

But:

> Ms. Borsky claims that she gives Lois lunch money every day, that she takes her to school in the morning, that she picks her up again in the afternoon, and that she supervises her homework every evening.

Judgment writing often features lists such as those of Ms. Borsky, above: lists of claims, lists of arguments, lists of facts, lists of accusations, lists of citations, lists of charges. As a structural device, therefore, parallelism is especially important.

To summarize:

1. Structure sentences to re-enforce meaning.

2. Create emphasis, remembering that the most emphatic position in a sentence is the end, the second most emphatic the beginning.

3. Use parallel structures for parallel ideas.

*   *   *

Exercises: Sentence Structure
Exercise Key, p. 101

Revise the following sentences, concentrating on clarifying and emphasizing meaning through structure. In some cases you might have to impose a specific meaning.

1. It was reasonable for the police officer to expect that the driver who had been involved in this type of motor vehicle accident—end over end—who had to be physically removed by emergency personnel, and at the same time, who had the odour of an alcoholic beverage on his breath, and the presence of alcohol bottles at the scene—all of which would lead a reasonable police officer to believe that medical staff would have obtained a sample of his blood for medical purposes.

2. This conclusion is based on the testimony of Mr. Loris who stated he left the defendant's vehicle to travel in another vehicle in search of alcohol and the absence of any statement by him that he took the keys and the defendant's admission that he retrieved keys from the police.

3. He argues that due diligence does not mean not depositing waste in the water, but that it means minimizing the impact of the waste by following the guidelines that are put in place, by doing it in a reasonable manner, as a reasonable man ought to minimize the effect of the impact.

4. What remained for determination was which party should have custody of the children of the marriage, what sum should be paid as maintenance for the children and the division of the matrimonial property.

5. Counsel for the accused, Mr. Seresa, argued that the wrong charge was laid, that is to say that this was theft by conversion rather than theft and also argued that there was doubt as to the ownership of the property in question and that it was not proved beyond a reasonable doubt that Custom Home Design was the owner of the subject property.

6. Her teacher claims that, most importantly, Carol's work has suffered through neglect since her mother has begun her new job, and her attendance has been irregular, and she has difficulty relating with her classmates.

7. When one has to deal with claims of breach of either common law or fiduciary care, it is not unusual to find that counsel for a big corporation tends to try and focus the attention of the court on the responsibility of the employee who deals with the particular matter rather than on that of the corporation as an entity.

8. Over and above the need any man has for counsel when asked to risk his last penny on even an apparently reasonable project, was the need here for informed advice as to whether there was any real chance of the company's affairs becoming viable if the documents were signed.

9. In regard to the evidence of the accused, Walter Tolley, I find him not to be a credible witness on this issue and reject his evidence beyond a reasonable doubt that he did not participate in the sale or negotiation of the sale of the property and also that he received a cheque payable to him in the amount of one thousand dollars and cashed that cheque and gave that one thousand dollars to Mr. Rice.

10. It is clear then that the thrust of the legislative response to this problem is to increase the probability of detection and to make the sanction more severe in order to discourage potential offenders.

CHAPTER 5

Words

"He words me, girls, he words me"
Antony and Cleopatra, 5.2.191

Nothing about the law gives satirists more opportunities for jokes than legal language. In *Gulliver's Travels* we learn that the laws of Brobdingnag "are expressed in the most plain and simple terms, wherein those people are not mercurial enough to discover above one interpretation." We can rest assured, therefore, that the problem of legal language was at least as severe in the eighteenth century as it is in the twenty-first.

When it comes to words alone, the main culprits in judgments are the passive voice, the verb "to be," Latin, jargon, and legalese. Let's examine each of these repeat offenders in turn.

The Passive Voice

Sentences take on life through active verbs, as becomes clear if we change the opening of this sentence from active into passive: life is taken on in sentences through active verbs. By definition, the passive voice is inert. Almost always, moreover, it is wordier than the active voice. Here is a typical example of the use of the passive in a judgment (the instances of the passive voice are italicized):

> She testified that it *was directed* by department guidelines that a referral of a matter from the audit branch to the special investigation branch *should be made* where a minimum of $15,000 in federal tax *was suspected* of being evaded.

We can breathe some life into that sentence by revising it as follows:

> She testified that department guidelines *directed* agents *to refer* a matter from the audit branch to the special investigation branch when they *suspected* federal tax evasion of more than $15,000.

To revise the sentence, I had to add the word "agent"; the active voice demands agency. It enhances vitality, brevity, and clarity.

If the active voice is so desirable, why use the passive, ever? Primarily for one reason: to avoid attributing agency. Politicians use the passive voice for this purpose because they are wily. If they respond to a fiasco by asserting that "mistakes were made," they create the impression of humility without admitting fault. We wait in vain for the phrase, "I made mistakes." Judges, of course, do not use the passive voice politically.

Judges are drawn into passivity by the nature of their work, in which agency is often unknown or irrelevant. Take, for example, the following sentence:

Constable Jones arrested the accused one block from the bank.

This is an active sentence: we know who did what to whom. Whenever possible, judges should write such sentences. Often, however, we do not know who made the arrest, or, more likely, who made the arrest is completely irrelevant. The point is the arrest, not who made it. So we find sentences like, "The accused was arrested one block from the bank." Once this habit is established, it becomes automatic, even when the name is known and relevant, to write, "The accused was arrested by Constable Jones one block from the bank." Potentially active sentences are allowed to be lethargic.

The moral? Be alert to the seductive power of the passive voice. Use the passive only for special reasons, as when agency is unknown or irrelevant.

The Verb "To Be"

The verb "to be" raises powerful emotions among writers, most of them negative. Although I have never substantiated the story, I heard once of a society in the United States dedicated to the eradication of the verb in all its manifestations. In certain moods I would not object, at least if I were allowed to make one exception: "To be or not to be, that is the question." The answer to Hamlet's question among sophisticated prose stylists, it seems, is "not 'to be'." Why?

Here are two examples:

He was in excess of his authority and his partner was in violation of the law.

The sentence can be revised as follows:

He exceeded his authority and his partner violated the law.

Although the verb "to be" does not obscure agency, it shares with the passive voice a flabby indirection and wordiness.

Jargon

The word "jargon" is ambiguous. In one sense, it means simply "the specialized vocabulary of a particular group or profession." In this sense, the word is neutral: jargon is neither good nor bad, simply a fact of life. Even hockey players use jargon. In another, negative sense, however, "jargon" means "meaningless talk or chatter." Jargon becomes a problem when a member of a specialized group tries to speak to outsiders.

The law cannot exist without jargon, and judges cannot deliver judgment without resort to it. Some legal terms and phrases, such as *habeas corpus* or *stare decisis*, represent complex and well established legal principles that cannot be made clear to the lay reader without a lengthy explanation. When such terms are necessary, the lay reader must turn to counsel for assistance, and this is as it should be; a judgment is not a legal textbook. Jargon of this kind is often called a term of art. One need not use terms of art very often, however, and sometimes even they can be coupled with a common English equivalent to give the lay reader the gist of the issue.

Terms of art provide the only excuse for Latin in judgments. In his 1981 address on judgment writing, former Chief Justice Brian Dickson asked "does the law need Latin? Does it need obsolete terms and phrases?" His answer was compelling: "the language of the law should be as dynamic as the society which the law seeks to serve." Since 1981, with a few exceptions, Latin phrases have become an endangered species in judgments, and even Greenpeace seems to have no desire to save them. Once we get rid of the few remaining survivors, such as *infra* (below) and *supra* (above), the world of judicial prose will be a more comfortable place for contemporary Canadians.

The pernicious species that continues to thrive in contemporary judgments is not legal jargon but legalese.

Legalese

Courtrooms are formal places. They are places with a carefully prescribed etiquette, a ceremonious manner of address, and a respect for tradition. Given this drift towards ceremony and formality, it is not surprising that one sometimes finds in the language of judgments an excessive formalism, a tendency towards stylistic elevation that verges on pomposity. The tendency is sometimes the result of long-standing custom in the law itself, but not always; sometimes it seems to come from the ingratiating efforts of courtroom visitors—litigants, police officers, expert witnesses, counsel—to be on their best verbal behaviour. An occasional lapse into this kind of vocabulary poses no real danger; habitual usage, however, results in a judicial voice that is artificially and unnecessarily remote from the common reader.

If you can find no legalese in any of the sentences below, you are probably a dangerous offender (the legalisms have been italicized):

1. The amount at issue was *in excess of* one hundred dollars. (Why not "more than"?).

2. The *said* letter was dated July 17, 1967. (In most cases "the letter" is perfectly clear; in others, use any cross-reference except "said").

3. The questioning *commenced* at 5:30 p.m. (Why not "began"?).

4. Inspector Barrett *attended at* the house as soon as his office was contacted. (Why not "went to"?).

Two of the offenders above—"said" and "attended at"—are so common in legal language that they have almost achieved the status of jargon. The two others, however, are found often in ordinary speech and would be unexceptionable if they were not usually symptoms of a more general linguistic inflation.

Here are some examples of legalistic expressions paired with their everyday equivalents:

adjacent to	next to
prescribed	set
necessitate	need
concerning	about
subsequently	later
prior to	before
provided that	if

Here are some examples of legalisms that can usually be replaced with plain language or, even better, deleted:

hereinafter—instead of "(hereinafter called 'Jones')" use "(Jones)"
aforesaid—omit or use "previously mentioned"
the within—omit or use "this"
herewith—instead of "enclosed herewith" use "I enclose"
pursuant to—instead of "pursuant to the terms" use "under the terms"
said (as adjective)—instead of "said contract" use "this contract"

The dangers of legalese should not lead judges to the lowest common denominator of word choice—to the average vocabulary, say, of the Canadian ten-year-old. Although some advocates of plain English seem attracted to such extreme limitations, they are doomed to fail in judgments; nor is there any reason to attempt them. The problem of legalese springs not so much from using a difficult vocabulary as from using one that is artificial and alienating—a vocabulary that warns readers they are on foreign and probably hostile terrain. The problem intensifies when legalese is combined with jargon.

* * *

Exercises: Verbs, Legalese, Jargon
Exercise Key, p. 103

Examine the following sentences for problems with the passive voice, the verb "to be," legalese, and jargon. Revise them accordingly.

1. The argument as applied to the instant case is, in essence, that prior to and at the time of the rezoning application the nature of the project was clearly understood to be a condominium development.

2. In those Orders the Learned Master granted a Rice Order in the within foreclosure Action which, *inter alia*, approved the offer to purchase of the Appellant for the mortgaged property.

3. Prior to May of 1988, Dynatech became dissatisfied with the performance of its then distributor.

4. The Crown advises this Court that the tape has in fact been lost.

5. The defence has made an application based on *Stinchcombe v. The Queen*, and it is for a stay of proceedings on the grounds of failure on the part of the Crown to provide full disclosure.

6. However, in the event that there is a non-compliance with the conditions attached to the probation order, recourse is possible to S.26 Y.O.A. for a new breach charge.

7. The diagnosis that the mother reported had been determined by the attending physician, was that the child had sustained a spiral fracture of the leg, resulting from an unexplained injury.

8. The meaning of said clause is fully explained in *Lassum v. The Queen* (*supra*, p.5).

9. The question is whether Star Brewery Ltd.(hereinafter referred to as "Star") took steps to avert the pollution of the stream.

10. The instant case, however, can be distinguished from *Payne v. The Queen*.

*   *   *

Prejudicial Language

When I first began to think about linguistic bias in relation to judicial writing, I came across a cartoon that still strikes me as wonderfully apt. A bald, bespectacled, walrus-mustached judge, garbed appropriately in black, sits in court staring down at a defendant, to whom he declares, "Surely not guilty. Next case." The defendant—bald, bespectacled, walrus-mustached— is his own self-image. No prejudice there. Clearly an unbiased judgment. The cartoonist need not have chosen a judge to make the point; no one is immune from prejudice, not even cartoonists, who are prone to stereotype their representations of judges. But the power of the courts lends an urgency to prejudicial judgment lacking in some other contexts. If an English professor shows bias, the results may harm the student but are unlikely to include a term in prison.

This chapter is not about prejudice in judgment but about prejudice in language. The two kinds of prejudice do not always coincide. We have all known individuals, I suspect, who are slyly political in their use of language but deeply prejudicial in their attitudes, and individuals who, locked into linguistic habits acquired in childhood, get tripped up on biased language but think and act in unbiased ways. The problem with language is that it carries a history of prejudice along with it; language itself is not disinterested. And since we cannot think and act without language, we must either allow it to sweep us along or attempt to re-direct its course.

Anyone who doubts the power of linguistic history need only read Shakespeare. One of the most terrifying lines in *Othello* occurs after Othello confesses the murder of Desdemona to Emilia, her lady-in-waiting. "'Twas I that kill'd her," he says. Emilia replies, "O, the more angel she, / And you the blacker devil." The sudden revelation of a deep racial loathing that Emilia has kept hidden throughout the play chills to the bone. For her, this noble black warrior has *always* been a black devil; his murder only intensifies his blackness. In expressing her hatred, Emilia draws on associations between blackness, ugliness, and the devil that have persisted in the English language since the Middle Ages.

Gender bias also appears in Shakespeare. Perhaps the subtlest instance in English of the notorious slippage between the gendered and ungendered use of the word "man" occurs in *Hamlet*. Hamlet's lines on the greatness of "man" are often quoted by humanists to epitomize the Renaissance celebration of *human* potential:

> What a piece of work is a man, how noble in reason, how infinite in faculty, in form and moving how express and admirable, in action how like an angel, in apprehension, how like a god—the beauty of the world, the paragon of animals!

Appreciations of this speech tend to overlook two things. First, it culminates in an expression of loathing. Secondly, and more importantly for our purposes, it ends with Hamlet acknowledging the ironic smiles of his auditors, Rosencrantz and Guildenstern, at his fixation on the word "man":

> And yet to me what is this quintessence of dust? Man delights not me—no, nor woman neither, though by your smiling you seem to say so.

By the end of the speech the "true" meaning of the word "man" has become clear. Although we may assume that the celebration of "man" refers to "human" potential, including both men and women, Hamlet and his fellow students take it to mean humans like them: men, not women. And history has tended to agree.

James Joyce called history a nightmare from which we cannot awake. The struggle to break free from a history of linguistic bias tends to take two different forms. On the one hand, we may argue that language merely reflects social reality, and that the way to change language is to change society. To worry about whether we use the word "chair" or the word "chairman" is from this perspective to put the cart before the horse. On the other hand, we may argue that language itself shapes social reality, that young girls bombarded with stereotypes of feminine beauty, say, are likely to grow up not only aspiring to fulfill these images but constricted by a society that expects them to do so. To worry about calling young women "dolls" is from this perspective to put the cart where it belongs.

The more sophisticated views of the relationship between language and society avoid being trapped by one or the other of these reductive extremes. Both arguments embody important partial truths. One need not overemphasize the significance of language as a molder of social reality to take its role seriously. Even if we say that actions speak louder than words, words still speak. And few would accept the proposition that sticks and stones will break our bones but words will never hurt us.

The lists of usage below may help to illustrate how hurtful words may be disarmed. Lists, however, are potentially dangerous: they go out of date rapidly, and they invite complacency. Given the rapidity of change in usage and the emotional volatility that accompanies it, perhaps the most useful advice is the most general: be endlessly alert to the issue of prejudicial language, keep up to date, test your own words for hidden biases, be sensitive to the needs of the people in court, and, whenever possible, involve them in your linguistic choices. The principle of sympathetic respect for all readers and listeners underlies the entire process of communication.

The suggestions under "A Miscellany" and "Race and Ethnicity" are adapted from *The Canadian Press Stylebook* (see the Reading List).

A MISCELLANY

1. Mention a disability only when it is pertinent.

2. When referring to a disability, be accurate. If *crippling arthritis is* the condition, do not be satisfied with the label *crippled*.

3. Avoid identifying people with their disabilities. Highlight the person, not the disability: not *the blind* but *people who are blind*.

4. In cases of AIDS, beware of creating the impression that only homosexuals are at risk.

5. If homosexuality is at issue, try to determine from the person involved the language of preference. *Gay* may be preferable to *homosexual*, and *gay women* to *lesbians*. Be careful of referring to *sexual preference*; *sexual orientation* is often felt to be more accurate.

6. Do not refer to someone as adopted unless it is pertinent.

7. When referring to someone who has been adopted, avoid using such terms as *real mother* or *real parents*; use instead *natural mother* or *birth mother*.

8. Do not refer to age unless it is pertinent. Be careful of the euphemistic *senior* or *senior citizen*. If the person is old and the information is relevant, say so.

9. Do not identify people by religion or national origin unless it is pertinent.

RACE AND ETHNICITY

1. Identify a person by race or ethnic group only if it is pertinent.

2. Do not use the term *Negro* unless the person prefers it. The term *black* is acceptable in North America generally, although *African-American* is sometimes preferred in the United States.

3. The word *Inuk* (plural *Inuit*) is preferred to *Eskimo*.

4. *First Nations' peoples, aboriginal peoples,* and *native peoples* are preferred to *Indians* for the original inhabitants of Canada.

5. Avoid racial and ethnic stereotyping, both explicit and implicit.

1. Avoid stereotyping according to fixed notions of male and female nature.

   EXAMPLE: She manages to be both feminine and professional at the same time.

2. Avoid stereotyping according to fixed notions of male and female roles.

   EXAMPLE: One must question whether her mother's job as a trucker provides an appropriate role model for Carol.

3. Avoid using language that demeans women.

   EXAMPLES: terms that identify women as sex objects — *bird, chick, babe, doll, tomato.*

4. Avoid treating wives as appendages of their husbands.

   EXAMPLES: Use *Ms.* unless you know the individual prefers otherwise. Do not identify a woman as *the wife of* unless the information is pertinent.

5. Avoid the use of *man* as a generic noun. Studies show that readers tend to imagine a male subject when it is used, despite the fact that they "know" it is gender neutral. Experience shows that it creates ambiguity. It can create absurdity: *Man, as a mammal, breast-feeds his young.* And it is easy to avoid. One can substitute such words or phrases as *humanity, people, persons, humans, human beings, society, the public, the community, adults.*

6. Avoid the generic use of *he.* Try recasting your sentence in the plural: Not *a lawyer earns his money the hard way* but *lawyers earn their money the hard way.* Or use *he or she* (or *she or he*), trying to avoid awkwardness: *education helps a child realize his or her potential.* Or avoid pronouns altogether: *a lawyer earns money the hard way.*

7. Avoid gratuitous references to women's physical appearance.

   EXAMPLE: Janet Fulton, an impeccably dressed and attractive school teacher, was arrested for shoplifting.

8. Try to use job titles that include both men and women or that provide equality between men and women.

   EXAMPLES: Poet   Poet (not poetess)
              Craftsman   Artisan or craftswoman or woodworker, metalworker

Businessman	Businesswoman or merchant or stockbroker
Policeman	Police officer
Mailman	Mail carrier

9. Throw grammar to the winds and use *they* as a singular pronoun: *Everybody should pay their taxes on time.* Not only is this the democratic thing to do (this is the way most of us speak and most students write, even after they are taught it is incorrect); it puts us in the company of the best writers. Oliver Goldsmith wrote, "Every person . . . now recovered their liberty"; Lawrence Durrell wrote, "You do not have to understand someone in order to love them"; and, yes, Shakespeare wrote, "God send everyone their heart's desire." The rule in question, moreover, was not introduced into English grammar until the eighteenth century, so it is hardly a rule of nature.

* * *

Exercises: Prejudicial Language
Exercise Key, p. 104

Revise the sentences below to remove prejudicial language. Assume in each case that identifications by race, ethnicity, gender, sexual orientation, physical ability, age, or adoptive status are pertinent.

1. He was among a number of intelligent Eskimos who graduated in 1967 from the University of Toronto.

2. Counsel argues that the claims of Jonathan's real father to custody should outweigh those of his adoptive father.

3. There is no question that he contributed to the problem by acting in an effeminate manner.

4. The contemporary judge will know how to approach these questions. He will be trained in the relevant branches of the law, and he will be alert to their social implications.

5. The spokesman for the Police Department explained that juvenile delinquency had increased dramatically along with the increase in working wives.

6. Despite their inability to control alcohol abuse on their own reservations, the Indians living in Northern British Columbia have been pressing their claims for self-government.

7. Throughout history, men have shown themselves to be innately litigious.

8. When a lawyer makes such a statement in court, he can almost certainly count on an objection from the other side.

9. The bus line does not acknowledge that cripples should receive assistance from drivers.

10. Once the men were tied up, the accused told the ladies to leave the room.

CHAPTER 6

Judicial Styles

"I am much deceived but I remember the style"
Love's Labor's Lost, 4.1.96

The word "style" tends to produce two contradictory reactions from judges. One I call the Gradgrindian, after Thomas Gradgrind, the brutal elementary school teacher in Dickens' *Hard Times*. Gradgrind is obsessed with facts and sees his students as little pitchers to be filled up with them. "What I want," he says, "is facts . . . facts alone are wanted in life." Applied to judicial writing, Gradgrind's attitude might be translated as, "I don't care about style—that's for poets or novelists or pedantical English professors. I'm a judge. What I care about is substance. Substance alone is wanted in judgments." The response is familiar, I suspect, and it contains a partial truth. Overall, however, it represents a misunderstanding of how style works.

The second common reaction to "style" I call the Polonian, after the character in *Hamlet*. Polonius is a man in love with fancy words. The Polonian syndrome often afflicts judges who have taken writing courses. One finds them smiling over their computers as they add decorative words and phrases to their judgments. An example of the Polonian attitude occurs in an introductory law text once used at the University of Victoria. In a chapter entitled "The Language of the Law," the author quotes the opening sentences of a famous judgment by Lord Denning: "It happened on April 19, 1964. It was bluebell time in Kent." Contrasting this opening with what one usually finds in judgments, the author admits that Lord Denning's approach is "perhaps a trifle less factually informative," but then suggests that "it comes as a welcome change to the jaded reader of law reports."

We may all sympathize with jaded readers of law reports. Being jaded readers of judgments ourselves, we are likely to yearn for bluebells as we stumble through the arid wastes of legal argument. But we should not want bluebells at the expense of facts. The infatuation with beautiful words and phrases distorts the idea of style as much as the infatuation with substance. The proper response to the Polonian syndrome is the one that Queen Gertrude makes to one of Polonius's flights of rhetoric: "more matter, and less art."

Although contradictory, the Gradgrindian and Polonian syndromes share a common error: they assume that style and substance are separate things and mutually exclusive. The lover of substance rejects style; the lover of style rejects substance—or at least is willing to do without it on occasion, for refreshment. Most people who have thought seriously about the relationship between style and substance, however, or between form and content, reject this separation of the two. In an address entitled "Law as Literature," for example, the eminent jurist Benjamin Cardozo argues for the union of form and content:

> Form is not something added to substance as a mere . . . adornment. The two are fused into a unity. The strength that is born of form and the feebleness that is born of the lack of form are in truth qualities *of* the substance. They are the tokens of the thing's identity. They make it what it is.

This is the opinion of an eminent judge, not of a poet (or of an English professor). If we think of style in this way, as the *shape* of substance, not as something opposed to it, we won't want to reject style as inappropriate to judicial writing or to cultivate it as a superficial kind of decoration.

So it is possible (and desirable) for judges to be fine writers and fine judges at the same time.

Justice Cardozo's notion of the unity of form and substance represents one powerful way of thinking about style—a way that sees style in relation to the matter of a particular argument. But style may be seen in other relationships as well. Classical rhetoricians, for example, relate style to occasion: a formal occasion demands a formal style, an informal occasion demands an informal style. And one may also see style in relation to the self. The reason we recognize "It was bluebell time in Kent" as Lord Denning is because the style *is* in some ways the man. Rhetoricians call the self that is created in writing a *persona*, a word that means *mask*. The word is useful, not because it suggests chicanery or deception, but because it makes clear that the writing self is not identical to the living self and that different modes of writing might project different kinds of selves. The way in which a style creates an impression of a self is the topic of this chapter.

To say that judicial style creates an impression of a self is not to say that judges have the same stylistic freedom as novelists, journalists, or even academic writers. A judgment is rarely a token of an author's identity, a means of self-expression. The facts of a case are not invented by the judge; neither is the law. The opinions expressed in a case are the judge's only in a very narrow sense, since they must follow precedent and established legal principles, whether the judge agrees with them or not. Judges, unlike novelists, write in chains. Despite these restrictions, however, stylistic choices remain. And the choices can be important.

Lecturers on judicial writing (this one included) tend to oversimplify the topic in two ways. First, we often imply that only one stylistic choice is possible—that between good and bad writing. Secondly, we often identify good writing with a single kind of style—what is usually called the plain style. The plain style has five main characteristics:

1. simple diction
2. spare use of figures of speech
3. short sentences
4. simple structures
5. transparency (the style does not call attention to itself)

I appreciate the plain style myself, especially for judges, who must aspire to clarity, conciseness, and coherence. But, even for judges, the plain style is not the only one available. And plainness itself may take many different forms.

To give some idea of the range of possible judicial styles, I have chosen four examples. All four of the passages are well written, although the more critically inclined will find they fall short of perfection. For each passage we will focus on a single question: what makes each style distinctive? What makes it possible for us to read a passage and say *that* is Justice Cardozo or Chief Justice Dickson or Lord Denning? To answer that question we will consider the stylistic elements listed above: diction, figures of speech, sentence structure, sentence length, and rhetorical effects that call attention to themselves.

Magisterial

I call the following passage magisterial:

> No one can study the vague and wavering statements of treaties and decision in this field of international law with any feeling of assurance at the end that he has chosen the right path. One looks in vain either for uniformity of doctrine or for scientific accuracy of exposition. There are wise cautions for the statesman. There are few precepts for the judge. All the more, in this uncertainty, I am impelled to the belief that until the political departments have acted, the courts, in refusing to give effect to treaties, should limit their refusal to the needs of the occasion; that they are not bound by any rigid formula to nullify the whole or nothing; and that in determining whether this treaty survived the coming of war, they are free to make choice of the conclusion which shall seem the most in keeping with the traditions of the law, the policy of the statutes, the dictates of fair dealing, and the honor of the nation.
>
> (Justice Cardozo, 1938)

What do I mean by a magisterial style?

Notice first of all the avoidance of the personal pronoun, the word "I." Instead of "I," we get "one," or "the judge"—impersonal forms that distance the self. When "I" is used, only once, its subjectivity is denied: "I am impelled." This is an "I" with no freedom of choice. This is an impersonal style, one that subordinates the self to the law. The judge, in a sense, is a mere conduit for the law, who speaks through him; the voice is not that of the person but of the law itself.

The choice of words, or diction, also marks this passage as magisterial. The vocabulary tends toward elevation, toward the Latinate, as in "assurance," "cautions," "precepts," "impelled," "nullify," "dictates." These are not especially obscure words—the effect is magisterial rather than pompous—but they are definitely formal and chosen partly for rhetorical effect. They aspire to dignity. Notice the difference between saying "I believe" and saying "I am impelled to the belief that." The sonority of the language re-enforces the strength of the assertion.

Perhaps the most striking characteristic of this style is its structural symmetry. This is a style that reflects a commitment to balance, harmony, rational order. Take the second sentence, for example:

> One looks in vain
> either for uniformity of doctrine
> or for scientific accuracy of exposition.

Or the third and fourth sentences:

> There are wise cautions for the statesman.
> There are few precepts for the judge.

The final sentence of this paragraph epitomizes the magisterial style. It is long, structurally complex, elaborately symmetrical, and self-consciously rhetorical. A schematic version might help to clarify how it works:

> All the more,
>   in this uncertainty,
> I am impelled to the belief
>   that until the political departments have acted,
>   the courts, in refusing to give effect to treaties,
>   should limit their refusal to the needs of the occasion;
>   that they are not bound by any rigid formula
>   to nullify the whole or nothing;
>   and that in determining whether this treaty
>   survived the coming of war, they are free to
>   make choice of the conclusion which shall seem
>   the most in keeping with
>   the traditions of the law,
>   the policy of the statutes,
>   the dictates of fair dealing,
>   and the honor of the nation.

This is rhetoric we call rhetorical. The sentence is tied together with elaborate parallelism, as indicated in the underlining of the word that; the parallel structure heightens clarity and enhances the sentence's rhythmic movement towards climax. The final four phrases of the sentence are so symmetrical that they might almost be scanned as verse. They are almost exactly equal in length, and they ascend in importance from the law and statutes to principles of fair dealing and the honour of the nation. The word "dictates" is chosen, I suspect, for the benefit of the alliteration in "dictates of fair dealing." A similar fondness for sound effects is found in the earlier phrase, "make choice of the conclusion." Why not "they are free to conclude"? Here Justice Cardozo chooses rhetorical effect over conciseness.

This, then, is a magisterial style. It is impersonal, elevated, authoritative, ceremonious. It aspires to power and dignity. Its effects are achieved at some cost to brevity and clarity. I suspect that most of us are not very attracted by this style and would probably call it old-fashioned. It *is* old-fashioned; styles reflect periods as well as personalities. But it is not old-fashioned merely as a style of writing. It is old-fashioned as a style of judging. It implies a relationship among judge, subject, and audience that probably seems too formal and distant for most contemporary judges. If you prefer a less magisterial style, it is probably because you prefer a less magisterial role for judges.

This preference for a less magisterial role can be seen in the next passage from former Chief Justice Dickson.

Formal

Each of these tests is helpful as far as it goes, but each is too general to provide a clear demarcation in concrete instances. This is shown by the variety of cases and the diversity of opinion in this case itself. To resolve the matter one must recall, I think, the policy basis of the rule against multiplicity and duplicity. The rule developed during a period of extreme formality and technicality in the preferring of indictments and laying of informations. It grew from the humane desire of Judges to alleviate the severity of the law in an age when many crimes were still classified as felonies, for which the punishment was death by the gallows. The slightest defect made an indictment a nullity. That age has passed. Parliament has made it abundantly clear in those sections of the *Criminal Code* having to do with the form of indictments and informations that the punctilio of an earlier age is no longer to bind us. We must look for substance and not petty formalities.

(Mr. Justice Dickson, 1978)

The formal style is most easily defined by contrast to the magisterial. Let's examine Chief Justice Dickson's most characteristic devices in relation to Justice Cardozo's.

In the use of the personal pronoun, Justice Cardozo's "I am impelled to the belief" may be contrasted with Chief Justice Dickson's "I think" in the fourth line. The phrase "I think," which, in less skillful writers becomes an obsessive "in my view," implies a conception of the law as complex, uncertain, filtered through the interpretation of fallible human beings, including himself. Notice, too, in this context, the pronouns in the next to the last line: "bind us"; "we must." Chief Justice Dickson's style reaches out to include his audience. His is not a distant voice from above. This, then, is a more personal and collaborative style than the magisterial.

Consider next the choice of words. Like Justice Cardozo, Chief Justice Dickson tends to use a rather elevated vocabulary: "demarcation," "alleviate," "nullity," "punctilio." He balances this formality, however, with informality. One of the most distinctive features of this passage is the wide range of vocabulary. In the first sentence, for example, the first half is informal, almost colloquial; the second half is formal—and its formality is heightened by the addition of alliteration in "clear demarcation in concrete instances." The word "punctilio" in the penultimate sentence was not chosen to please the more puritanical of the plain stylists. It sends some of us to our dictionary. But it is very well chosen. It reproduces stylistically the very point Chief Justice Dickson wants to make about the law: times change, and the forms of one age are not appropriate to another. Chief Justice Dickson, like Justice Cardozo, makes occasional demands on his audience.

Both writers share as well a fondness for syntactical symmetry. Chief Justice Dickson, however, uses the device much less ostentatiously than Justice Cardozo. He is careful not to let his style call attention to itself. Consider, for example, the final sentence: "we must look for substance and not petty formalities." This could have been written, and might have been, by Justice Cardozo, "we must look for substance; we must not look for petty formalities," or, "we must look not for petty formalities but for substance." Chief Justice Dickson avoids this kind of studied rhetorical effect.

Chief Justice Dickson avoids as well Justice Cardozo's use of long and complicated sentences to build towards climactic effects. Although his sentences are sometimes long, they are rarely very complicated in structure. Chief Justice Dickson pursues variety in length and structure, not cumulative rhetorical impact. This can be seen in the variations in length and structure in the final four sentences, beginning with "the slightest defect made an indictment a nullity."

Chief Justice Dickson's is thus a formal style. It shares elements in common with Justice Cardozo's style, but it is more personal, less elevated, less authoritative, less ceremonious. The persona that emerges through this style is not that of a master (*magister*) through whom the law speaks but that of a highly trained professional sensitive to the difficulties of the subject under consideration and conscious of the need to persuade an audience.

Informal

> To say it would be common knowledge to most people that feet are at risk in circumstances like the present does not advance the defendant's position very far. At risk? Perhaps so. But the risk of injury is not the same as actual injury. Without the precipitating occurrence of the accident, the plaintiff might have gone to the end of her life without an amputation. And since Dr. Moorhouse invoked "common knowledge . . . (of) most people", I am emboldened to suggest that it is common knowledge that many people have diabetes but only a few of them have amputations. Surely in statistical terms the number of diabetic persons who have to suffer an amputation must be but a minor fraction of the total group. To say that the plaintiff, without an accident to her foot, would very likely have developed gangrene, necessitating an amputation, is to substitute speculation for reason and guesswork for proof.
>
> (Mr. Justice Freedman 1980)

Differences between formal and informal styles, of course, are differences of degree. Let's consider the qualities that make Mr. Justice Freedman's style less formal than Chief Justice Dickson's or Justice Cardozo's.

Like Chief Justice Dickson, Mr. Justice Freedman allows a personal voice to enter his prose, but he does so far more directly. Notice how he reaches out to engage his audience with the rhetorical question and answer: "At risk? perhaps so." Notice too the self-revelation that bubbles through the ironic tone, as in "I am emboldened to suggest." The use of an old-fashioned word like "emboldened" heightens the irony.

Mr. Justice Freedman's vocabulary is less formal than Chief Justice Dickson's, and he stays within a narrower range. He uses Latinate words when they are appropriate, as in "precipitating occurrence" and "speculation." But he also uses a simple, colloquial word like "guesswork." And he uses words for witty and ironic effects, as in the case of "emboldened" and the playful contrast between "speculation" and "guesswork."

The most distinctive feature of this passage is its variety of sentence structure. Mr. Justice Freedman shifts his structures from sentence to sentence. The first sentence begins with an infinitive construction: "to say." The second and third sentences take the form of question and answer. The fourth sentence begins with a conjunction. The fifth sentence begins with a long introductory phrase. And so it goes. This variety of sentence structure creates the passage's most remarkable effect—its lively, conversational tone.

This, then, is an informal style. Although not exactly colloquial, the style moves in that direction. It is more personal than either Justice

Cardozo's or Chief Justice Dickson's. It even edges towards familiarity with the audience in its ironic wit. It is a forceful style but not elevated or ceremonious. The persona it creates is brisk, impatient of nonsense, familiar, even a bit playful.

Artful Plain

> Now let me say at once that in the vast majority of cases a customer who signs a bank guarantee or a charge cannot get out of it. No bargain will be upset which is the result of the ordinary interplay of forces. There are many hard cases which are caught by this rule. Take the case of a poor man who is homeless. He agrees to pay a high rent to a landlord just to get a roof over his head. The common law will not interfere. It is left to Parliament. Next take the case of a borrower in urgent need of money. He borrows it from the bank at high interest and it is guaranteed by a friend. The guarantor gives his bond and gets nothing in return. The common law will not interfere. Parliament has intervened to prevent moneylenders charging excessive interest. But it has never interfered with banks.
>
> (Lord Denning, 1974)

Finally, the style of Lord Denning, the judicial writer the textbooks turn to when they want examples of fine judicial prose. What are the distinctive characteristics of Lord Denning's style?

If Justice Cardozo's style is impersonal, Chief Justice Dickson's personal, and Mr. Justice Freedman's familiar, Lord Denning's, we might say, is blunt: "now let me say at once." The tone is assertive, brusque, no-nonsense.

If Mr. Justice Freedman's vocabulary is relatively informal, Lord Denning's verges on the colloquial—as in "cannot get out of it," "hard cases," "take the case of." Only words like "interplay" and "intervened" keep this language in the courts and out of the marketplace. Lord Denning does not use slang, but he likes to roll up his sleeves.

If Justice Cardozo's sentence structure reminds us of Henry James, Lord Denning's reminds us of Hemingway. Curt, simple sentences are his trademark. Because of this, and because of his simple diction, we might want to call Lord Denning's style a plain style. But it is not really plain at all. It is as carefully crafted and artificial as Justice Cardozo's style. The bluntness and plainness are so contrived that they call attention to themselves. This artificial quality emerges clearly in a schematic version of the passage:

> Now let me say at once
> > that in the vast majority of cases a customer who signs a bank guarantee or a charge cannot get out of it.
> No bargain will be upset which is the result of the ordinary interplay of forces.
> There are many hard cases which are caught by this rule.

(a) Take the case of a poor man who is homeless.
  (b) He agrees to pay a high rent to a landlord just to get a roof over his head.
  (c) The common law will not interfere.
  (d) It is left to Parliament.
(a) Next take the case of a borrower in urgent need of money.
  (b) He borrows it from the bank at high interest and it is guaranteed by a friend.
  (b) The guarantor gives his bond and gets nothing in return.
  (c) The common law will not interfere.
  (d) Parliament has intervened to prevent moneylenders charging excessive interest.
  (d) But it has never interfered with banks.

Notice the elaborate symmetries, which I have highlighted by alphabetical labels. This plain style is as artfully composed as a sonnet.

The effect of Lord Denning's style is somewhat surprising. Because of its plainness, we might want to say that Lord Denning's style is that of the common person, the average citizen. It seems simple, direct, clear, homespun. But its commonness is of a special kind. The voice I hear through this style is not that of the average citizen but that of an urbane and sophisticated writer, playing at being plain. Lord Denning's style, then, is not a plain but an artful plain style.

———

A few concluding remarks. As we discovered earlier, a judicial writing style is not entirely a matter of choice. It is dictated in part by the occasion, by the needs of a specific audience, by the material, by the judicial role. It is also dictated, of course, more subtly, by habit, by unconscious preferences, and by the times. The passages we have examined show clearly, however, that there are choices to make, and that the choices mean something—they are not mere matters of decoration. A choice of a style implies something important about one's relation to the subject at hand, to the audience, and to the judicial role. In this sense style creates a persona, represents a self. To adapt a remark of Ben Jonson's, "language most shows a [judge]; write that I may see thee."

*   *   *

83

Exercises: Judicial Styles
Exercise Key, p. 105

Developing a personal style requires alertness to the range of linguistic options available. The following exercises, therefore, ask you to experiment with different kinds of styles and different voices. Doing so should increase your sensitivity to stylistic effects and your awareness of the kind of style you would like to achieve.

1. *Reproduced below is the passage from Lord Denning that we have already examined. Test the differences between a plain style and an artful plain style by rewriting the passage in a plain style. When finished, ask yourself which version you prefer.*

Now let me say at once that in the vast majority of cases a customer who signs a bank guarantee or a charge cannot get out of it. No bargain will be upset which is the result of the ordinary interplay of forces. There are many hard cases which are caught by this rule. Take the case of a poor man who is homeless. He agrees to pay a high rent to a landlord just to get a roof over his head. The common law will not interfere. It is left to Parliament. Next take the case of a borrower in urgent need of money. He borrows it from the bank at high interest and it is guaranteed by a friend. The guarantor gives his bond and gets nothing in return. The common law will not interfere. Parliament has intervened to prevent moneylenders charging excessive interest. But it has never interfered with banks. *(153 words)*

2. *Reproduced below is the passage from Chief Justice Dickson that we have already examined. Test the differences between the formal style and the magisterial style by rewriting the passage in the magisterial style. When finished, ask yourself which version you prefer.*

Each of these tests is helpful as far as it goes, but each is too general to provide a clear demarcation in concrete instances. This is shown by the variety of cases and the diversity of opinion in this case itself. To resolve the matter one must recall, I think, the policy basis of the rule against multiplicity and duplicity. The rule developed during a period of extreme formality and technicality in the preferring of indictments and laying of informations. It grew from the humane desire of Judges to alleviate the severity of the law in an age when many crimes were still classified as felonies, for which the punishment was death by the gallows. The slightest defect made an indictment a nullity. That age has passed. Parliament has made it abundantly clear in those sections of the *Criminal Code* having to do with the form of indictments and informations that the punctilio of an earlier age is no longer to bind us. We must look for substance and not petty formalities. *(172 words)*

3. *The following passage, a modified original, is stylistically typical of many judgments. The style gestures towards formality on the one hand and informality on the other. Revise the passage twice: once accentuating the formal possibilities, and a second time accentuating the informal possibilities.*

The issue before me is whether it is in Joan's best interests to remain permanently with the Society by way of a Crown wardship without access, which may eventually lead to her adoption, or to return to the care of her father.

In deciding which of these two options is in Joan's best interests on a status review application, the enumerated criteria found in sections 65(1) (criteria on status review) and in 37(3) (best interests test) of the *Child and Family Services Act* (C.F.S.A.) must be weighed, keeping in mind all the while the declarations of principles found in section one of the C.F.S.A. Of particular importance are sections 1(a) and (b) that reinforce the need to respect the integrity of the family and to keep the family unit intact where at all possible and yet consistent with the best interests of the child. That this is the legislative test to be applied on a status review application was recently confirmed in the Supreme Court of Canada decision, *Catholic Children's Aid Society of Metropolitan Toronto v. Cidalia M. (187 words)*

CHAPTER 7

Revising

"And when it's writ, for my sake read it over"
Two Gentlemen of Verona, 2.1.130

The eighteenth-century writer, Samuel Johnson, advised authors to keep their writing in a desk for a year before deciding to publish it. Good advice for writers, but not for judges, who, like Hamlet, must worry about "the law's delay." Even if Johnson's advice cannot be taken literally, however, it is instructive nonetheless. Letting a piece of writing sit unread for a year achieves one significant effect: it transforms the author into an audience. Having lost all knowledge of a case, you become a genuine reader, and you ask yourself, "what could I possibly have meant by that"? This is the state of mind that must be at least imagined in order to revise effectively.

How does one achieve that mental state within days, hours, or even minutes of first composition? With difficulty. It helps, I think, to start with the negative, with what doesn't work. When my daughter was in grade seven, she came to me with the first draft of a report she had written. I read it, told her it was a promising start, and suggested she revise it. She returned about twenty minutes later with the report unchanged. "What happened to the revisions?" I asked. "Oh," she said, "I read it all the way through and couldn't find anything wrong." Unknowingly, she had followed the letter of the law: the word "revise" means simply "see again." It hadn't occurred to her that the point of "revision" was not merely to "see again" but to "see afresh," to "re-think."

To revise, then, does not mean merely re-reading a judgment with unfocused attention. If you look for nothing, you will find it, especially when the details of a case are still so familiar that the trees overwhelm the wood. To revise effectively, you must divide the task, focusing on specific questions. The nature of the questions and the order in which they are asked will vary from person to person. If you are conscious of some tendencies you want to resist in your writing, for example, you might put them in a checklist, to be consulted each time you write. I have included an example of a general checklist at the end of this section.

To give a rough idea of how the process of revision might work, let me divide it into six stages, focusing on the kinds of questions that might be posed at each stage. The division into distinct stages is somewhat misleading, of course, for in reality the stages will overlap considerably. Let's assume that we have before us the first draft of a judgment, in the usual structure: introduction, summary of facts, argument, and conclusion. Where do we go from here?

Stage One

This is the moment for shifting gears, for re-directing your attention from the needs of the material to the needs of an audience. Think first of your audience. Who are they? Remember the general needs we considered in Chapter 1. Are there special audiences for this judgment? Are there issues, even words, that might trigger violent emotional responses? Do you really want to call a disciplined non-violent march of protest an "illegal public tantrum"? Try to put yourself, in short, into the shoes of your readers, achieving imaginatively the effect of distance that would be automatic if you had the luxury of hiding your judgment in a drawer for a year.

Stage Two

Read your introduction. Ask yourself three questions: (1) have I identified the parties? (2) have I identified the nature of the case? (3) have I stated the issue or issues?

If the answer to these questions is yes, proceed to stage three; if the answer to the third question is no, then more analyzing and writing for discovery are in order.

Stage Three

Read through the entire judgment quickly, with the issue or issues firmly in mind. As you read, jot down a retrospective outline. Then ask yourself whether the sections of the judgment are in the most effective order. Is the overall structure clear? Is the order of arguments logical and persuasive?

Stage Four

Skim the entire judgment again, this time with a meat cleaver in hand. You have already stated the issues and structured the judgment; now you can cut out the fat. Have I included more facts than are necessary? Have I wandered into side issues? Have I belaboured the obvious? Have I quoted too much?

Stage Five

Re-write the judgment, as necessary. Focus on the clarity of the issues, the organization of the argument, and conciseness. Don't be too finicky about style; many sentence problems will disappear as you clarify, organize, and—a wonderful cure for sentence ills—cut.

Stage Six

Clean up the language. Focus on mechanics and style. Be conscious of habitual problems. Be conscious of your persona. When you see an unusually long sentence, take a second look.

The problem with revision, I have been told more than once, is time. The problem with writing, I have replied more than once, is time. If you desire to write well, you must revise. Fine writers, like Chief Justice Dickson and Lord Denning, tell us they revise and revise and revise. Here is Lord Denning's account of how he acquired his skill as a writer: "In chambers, if asked to advise, I took infinite pains in the writing of an opinion. I crossed out sentence after sentence. I wrote them again and again"(*The Discipline of the Law*, p. 7). When he delivered his 1981 address on judgment writing, Chief Justice Dickson said he tried to revise each judgment about seven times.

My suggestions for revision, I hope you will have noticed, attempt to be realistic. Thinking, skimming, cutting, polishing—these can move along quickly. They can go on forever, of course, even beyond Chief Justice Dickson's seven drafts, but they need not. A second draft is unlikely to achieve elegance, but a first draft is unlikely to achieve clarity, conciseness, and coherence. And the difference between a first draft, written as an act of discovery, and a second draft, written as an act of communication, can be dramatic.

Checklist for Reasons

A. Introduction

    1. Have I identified the parties?

    2. Have I explained the nature of the proceedings?

    3. Have I stated the central issue or issues?

B. Facts

    1. Have I pruned away irrelevant facts?

    2. Have I stated the facts clearly and in a logical order?

    3. Have I distinguished between the testimony and my findings?

    4. Have I dealt with the issue of credibility?

C. Argument

    1. Have I announced in advance the issue or issues?

    2. Have I arranged the issues in a logical order?

    3. Have I argued each issue in relation to the facts and the law?

    4. Have I pruned away any extraneous issues?

    5. Have I quoted documents unnecessarily or at unnecessary length?

D. Conclusion

    1. Is my conclusion clear?

    2. Does my conclusion follow logically from the argument?

APPENDIX 1

Exercise Key

"Your answer, sir, is enigmatical"
Much Ado About Nothing, 5.4.27

Chapter 1: Introductions
Exercises, p. 19

A. ASSESSING INTRODUCTIONS

1. *A successful version of the narrative-charge-issue introduction. The narrative is brief and vivid, the charge flows naturally out of it, and the issue is framed clearly and precisely. Notice the effective use of quotations.*

2. *An effective introduction to an appeal court judgment. The introduction includes, clearly and concisely, a great deal of contextual information: the nature of the appeal, the relevant parts of the* Labour Code *and the* Charter, *the essential facts, the nature of the grievance, and the issues to be determined. One might question the placement of the second sentence: could it go elsewhere with equal or better effect? And what about the legalistic doublet, "force and effect"? Why not simply "force"? Or simply "effect"?*

3. *An introduction that effectively incites curiosity. The recitation of convictions supports the idea that sentencing should be simple, and the statement of a complication in the* Criminal Code *whets the appetite: what kind of a complication could bear on such a case? The issue, however, is merely hinted at, not stated directly. One needs a crisp statement of the problem: what is the complication? That statement might be provided in the next sentence or two.*

4. *The opening lines of U.S. Supreme Court Justice Harry A. Blackmun's dissent from an order denying review in a Texas death penalty case. The example shows how introductions are determined in part by audience and occasion. Blackmun works slowly towards his statement of the issues, creating an emotional context for his dissent. Introductions like this are appropriate for high courts and broad issues.*

5. *The issue in this judgment appears in the second paragraph, which is not quoted. Knowing this, we cannot fault the opening for the lack of an issue-statement. We can fault it, however, for inducing vertigo. This head-spinning sentence provides a good example of over-compression: everything we need is there, but what does it mean? The sentence must be divided for the sake of clarity.*

6. *Lord Denning, of course. Notice the clarity and simplicity of the exposition, which culminates in a clear, if indirect, statement of the issue. Notice too that this introduction works to create sympathy for the little guy, Mr. Deeble. The sympathy works to humanize not only Mr. Deeble but Lord Denning, creating a compassionate image of the self. No matter how he decides, we will know that Lord Denning cares.*

B. FOUR VERSIONS OF AN INTRODUCTION

1. Claim-Narrative-Issue

Revenue Canada seeks to recover $67,000 in back taxes from L.M. Inc., on the ground that the deduction of business expenses incurred for the use of a yacht is disallowed by the *Income Tax Act*, Section 18(1)(1).Stats.Can.1970-71-72,c.63.

The vessel in question is the *Seawind*, built in 1947 as a tugboat. In 1981, it was refurbished and converted to its present use as the sole residence of its owners, Mr. and Mrs. Randolph, who charter it on occasion for fishing and for parties. The boat now features a large and comfortable lounge and a galley specializing in exotic cuisine. Its cabins accommodate 14 for overnight charters. In both 1985 and 1986, L.M. Inc. hired the boat to entertain guests.

The issue to be determined is whether the *Seawind* is a yacht.

2. Claim-Issue-Narrative

Revenue Canada seeks to recover $67,000 in back taxes from L.M. Inc., on the ground that the deduction of business expenses incurred for the use of a yacht is disallowed by the *Income Tax Act*, Section 18(1)(1).Stats.Can.1970-71-72,c.63. L.M. Inc. agrees that the *Income Tax Act* disallows expenses incurred in hiring yachts. It argues, however, that the boat it hired is not a yacht.

The vessel in question is the *Seawind*, built in 1947 as a tugboat. In 1981, it was refurbished and converted to its present use as the sole residence of its owners, Mr. and Mrs. Randolph, who charter it on occasion for fishing and for parties. The boat now features a large and comfortable lounge and a galley specializing in exotic cuisine. Its cabins accommodate 14 for overnight charters. In both 1985 and 1986, L.M. Inc. hired the *Seawind* to entertain guests.

3. Narrative-Claim-Issue

In 1981 Mr. and Mrs. Randolph converted an old tugboat, the *Seawind*, into a vessel that could serve both as their sole residence and as a source of income from group charters for fishing and parties. In making the conversion, they removed the boat's winch and installed a large and comfortable lounge, cabin accommodation for 14, and a galley specializing in exotic cuisine. Since 1981 the boat has been chartered on weekends, holidays, and for longer periods during the six weeks of Mr. Randolph's vacation from his regular job.

In 1985 and 1986, L.M., Inc. hired the *Seawind* to entertain guests. The company deducted the cost of these rentals from its taxes as a business expense: $20,000 in 1985, and $47,000 in 1986.

Revenue Canada now seeks to recover these amounts, on the ground that the *Income Tax Act* disallows business deductions "for the use or maintenance of property that is a yacht, a camp, a lodge or a golf course"(Section 18(1)(1).Stats.Can.1970-71-72,c.63).

The issue to be determined is whether this converted tugboat is a yacht.

4. Issue-Claim-Narrative

The issue in this case is whether the *Seawind*, a converted tugboat, is a yacht. Revenue Canada claims that it is, and that therefore the cost of its rental cannot be deducted as a business expense under the *Income Tax Act*; the *Act* disallows the deduction of expenses incurred "for the use or maintenance of property that is a yacht, a camp, a lodge or a golf course" (Section 18(1)(1).Stats.Can.1970-71-72,c.63).

The *Seawind* was built in 1947 as a tugboat. In 1981, it was refurbished and converted to its present use as the sole residence of its owners, Mr. and Mrs. Randolph, who charter it on occasion for fishing and for parties. The boat now features a large and comfortable lounge and a galley specializing in exotic cuisine. Its cabins accommodate 14 for overnight charters.

In both 1985 and 1986, L.M. Inc. hired the *Seawind* to entertain guests. In both years the company deducted from its taxes the cost of the rental, a total of $67,000, as a business expense.

Chapter 2: Organization
Exercises, p. 31

A. ORGANIZING THE FACTS

George Wilson faces two charges of assault arising out of events that occurred on December 1995 in the City of Warwick. Mr. Wilson is alleged to have struck Louise Mercer on the face with a cigarette in a bar and, later, to have pushed her into a tricycle on the landing outside the apartment where he lived with his wife, Beverly Brown. Mr. Wilson denies both charges. The issue is whether the evidence proves Mr. Wilson's guilt beyond a reasonable doubt.

The events in the bar began when Mr. Wilson, having consumed at least five beers, took offence at a remark by Ms. Mercer, the cocktail waitress and a social friend, criticizing his conduct with an exotic dancer. Mr. Wilson became angry and told Ms. Mercer to call "Bev," his wife. She did so. While she stood behind the bar holding the telephone, Mr. Wilson, angry and yelling, was leaning over the bar. He flicked a cigarette in her direction. The question is whether Mr. Wilson flicked his cigarette in anger at Ms. Mercer. Ms. Mercer claims that he did so, and that the cigarette hit her in the cheek; Mr. Wilson claims that he merely flicked his cigarette over the bar in frustration and that it did not hit Ms. Mercer but the bottles behind her.

Ms. Mercer's exact position holding the phone is in doubt; the differences in testimony on this point, however, are immaterial. More relevant is the testimony of witnesses, all of whom agree that Mr. Wilson was angry and flicked his cigarette in the direction of Ms. Mercer. Although Mr. Ronson, Mr. Wilson's friend, testified that the cigarette did not hit Ms. Mercer, he too agreed that Mr. Wilson flicked it in her general direction.

Ms. Mercer's position also finds support from the nature of the telephone conversation she had with Ms. Brown. Ms. Mercer testified that she informed Ms. Brown that Mr. Wilson had just hit her in the face with a cigarette and that she intended to phone the police to complain. Although Ms. Brown denied hearing that Ms. Mercer had been struck in the face, she admitted hearing that Ms. Mercer intended to call the police to complain about Mr. Wilson's actions. It is unreasonable to believe that Ms. Brown would know that Ms. Mercer intended to complain to the police without also knowing why she intended to complain.

Ms. Mercer's account of the event is also supported by the testimony of George Athopolis, who lives with Ms. Mercer. Mr. Athopolis saw Mr. Wilson lean over and flip his cigarette at Ms. Mercer, although he could not see whether it hit her because another person blocked his line of sight. He also saw Ms. Mercer holding her cheek afterwards. At this point he stood beside Mr. Wilson and heard him say, "Keep your bitch girl friend in line." He also heard Mr. Wilson call Ms. Mercer a number of unsavory names, to which she responded that Mr. Wilson was an alcoholic and did not deserve his beautiful wife and children.

Having considered all of the evidence cited above, I find as a fact that Mr. Wilson was angry with Ms. Mercer when he leaned over the bar; that he flicked the cigarette at her; that Ms. Mercer was hit by the cigarette, either directly or by ricochet from the bottles; and that Ms. Mercer informed Ms. Brown that she been hit on the cheek. Mr. Wilson is therefore guilty of the first charge of assault.

The second charge derives from an event alleged to have occurred later in the same evening, when Ms. Mercer, having taken some cigarettes to Ms. Brown at her request, was leaving the Brown/Wilson apartment. Both women heard Mr. Wilson returning home. Ms. Mercer claims that she then mounted the stairs from the apartment and met Mr. Wilson on the narrow landing, where he shoved her into a parked tricycle. Mr. Wilson denies shoving Ms. Mercer into the tricycle and claims instead that he met Ms. Mercer on the stairs, not the landing.

Ms. Mercer's testimony is supported by the implausibility of Mr. Wilson's account and by the testimony of Ms. Brown. Mr. Wilson claims that, although concerned about Ms. Mercer because she had already reported him to the police, he did not wait for her to climb to the top of the stairs but started down the stairs and passed her on the staircase. Ms. Brown, however, who was excluded from the testimony in the court, testified that Mr. Wilson met Ms. Mercer on the landing; Ms. Brown's preoccupation with her four-year-old on the stairs, however, prevented her from seeing what happened. I therefore find as fact that Mr. Wilson met Ms. Mercer on the landing and pushed her into the tricycle.

Mr. Wilson is therefore guilty of the second charge of assault.

This revision divides the narrative so that each charge can be considered singly. The division is not marked by headings, although it could be. For each charge, the revision provides an overview of the discrepancy in testimony and then incorporates the narrative into an argument about credibility. The original uses 1054 words; the revision uses 796 and still needs pruning.

B. ORGANIZING AN ARGUMENT

To exclude the evidence in this case, I must conclude that its admission would bring the administration of justice into disrepute. To arrive at that conclusion, I must first consider the questions established by the Supreme Court of Canada in *R. v. Collins* 33 C.C.C. (3d) 1: (1) would admission of the evidence make the trial unfair? (2) was the violation of rights under the

Charter serious? (3) if trivial, would the violation nonetheless bring the administration of justice into disrepute? In this instance the central question is the fairness of the trial.

In determining fairness, the Supreme Court distinguishes between real evidence and self-incriminatory evidence. The Court has held consistently that the admission of real evidence will generally not make a trial unfair, but the admission of self-incriminatory evidence will; see, in particular, Justice Iacobucci's statement in *R. v. Elshaw* (1991) 67 C.C.C. (3d) 97, at page 129. The evidence in this case, acquired as the result of a roadside screening test for alcohol, is self-incriminatory. Although in itself incapable of proving the guilt or innocence of the accused, it legitimized the demand that the accused provide a breath sample pursuant to s. 254(3). To admit such evidence would render the trial unfair and bring the administration of justice into disrepute. I therefore exclude the evidence and acquit the accused.

The structure of the original is as follows:

1. *Three factors are to be considered*
2. *The exclusion of evidence is not automatic*
3. R. v. Collins *establishes three factors*
4. *Real evidence and self-incrimination are different in relation to fairness*
5. *Self-incrimination is relevant to this case*
6. R. v. Elshaw *emphasizes the importance of self-incrimination*
7. *The question of fairness applies generally to all cases*
8. *In this case the breath samples were a key factor*
9. *The police followed common practice*
10. *Admission of the evidence creates unfairness*
11. *Unfairness brings the administration of justice into disrepute*
12. *Acquittal*

The structure of the revision is as follows:

1. *The test: disrepute must be established in relation to three questions*
2. *The central question is fairness*
3. *Real evidence and self-incrimination are different in relation to fairness*
4. *Self-incrimination is relevant to this case*
5. *Admission of the evidence creates unfairness*
6. *Unfairness brings the administration of justice into disrepute*
7. *Acquittal*

Re-structuring the argument improves not only its clarity but its conciseness. The original has 698 words, the revision 226.

Chapter 3: Conciseness
Exercises, p. 40

CONCISENESS IN QUOTATIONS

2.   The applicants' main argument is that insufficient information has been disclosed about the informant(s) against them. The lack of information is particularly damaging, they contend, for two reasons: first, because the allegations of a plot are serious and secondly, because the evidence needed to support or refute the allegations is unavailable. Without such information, according to the applicants, they are at the mercy of any inmate who concocts a plausible story.

Both a judgment of the Federal Court of Appeal and the *Corrections and Conditional Release Act* S.C. 1992, c. 20 lend support to the applicants' position by strictly limiting the right of authorities to withhold information about informants. In *Marco v. Regional Transfer Board and Smith* (1990), Mr. Justice Kilroy stated that "the burden is always on the authorities to demonstrate that they have withheld only such information as is strictly necessary for the purpose of protecting the safety of the informer." "In the final analysis," he concluded, "the test must be not whether there exist good grounds for withholding information but rather whether enough information has been revealed to allow the person concerned to answer the case against him" (2 F.C. 37 at 66-67). Although the *Corrections and Conditional Release Act* permits the withholding of information in certain circumstances, it places strict limits on such an action:

> 27.(3) ... where the Commissioner has reasonable grounds to believe that disclosure of information under subsection (1) or (2) would jeopardize
> (a) the safety of any person,
> (b) the security of a penitentiary, or
> (c) the conduct of any lawful investigation,
> the Commissioner may authorize the withholding from the offender of as much information as is strictly necessary in order to protect the interest identified in paragraph (a), (b), or (c).

It is clear, then, that the burden lies on the authorities to justify what information they withhold and why.

In this case, the authorities did not meet that test. The affidavit filed by Stuart Reese, an employee of Correctional Service Canada, states that summaries were made of documents which "by their disclosure could reveal the identity of confidential informants"(#7 and #8) but does not purport to have applied the appropriate criteria when reviewing whether additional information could have been provided to the applicants.

In addition to reducing the quotations, I have attempted to clarify the argument by re-structuring it. Some writers might divide my second paragraph. The gain in conciseness is significant: the original was 538 words; the revision is 386—for a savings of 28%.

Chapter 4: Paragraphs and Sentences

PARAGRAPH *Exercises, p. 46*

1. *Information of this kind, which becomes frustrating if treated in a series of single-sentence paragraphs, can be presented in two ways: in a developed paragraph or in a clearly announced list. Both possibilities are offered below.*

(a)   Although they live with their mother and attend school every day, the girls have a complicated after-school schedule. They spend Mondays with their mother. On Tuesdays Jane goes to their mother but Rebecca visits their father until 9:00 p.m. On Wednesdays, both girls go to their father, who keeps them overnight and delivers them to school the next morning. On Thursdays Rebecca goes to their mother, while Jane visits their father until 9:00 p.m. On Fridays both girls go to their maternal grandparents, who keep them until Saturday noon. They spend the rest of the weekend with their mother.

(b)   Although they live with their mother and attend school every day, the girls have a complicated after-school schedule:

Monday: Both girls stay with their mother.
Tuesday: Jane stays with their mother. Rebecca visits their father until 9:00 p.m.
Wednesday: Both girls stay overnight with their father, who delivers them to school the next morning.
Thursday: Rebecca stays with their mother. Jane visits their father until 9:00 p.m.
Friday: Both girls go to their maternal grandparents, who keep them until Saturday noon.
Saturday: Both girls return to their mother Saturday noon.
Sunday: Both girls stay with their mother.

2.   The evidence does not show that Ms. Cotton failed to address this matter in her affidavit because she desired to frustrate Mr. Rivers' access to Joseph. It is true that before the end of 1989 Ms. Cotton did not permit Joseph to stay overnight with Mr. Rivers. She swears in her affidavit that she did not permit overnight access because of certain sexual practices of Mr. Rivers; since she refuses to specify the nature of these practices, however, I am unable to assess the reasonableness of her conclusion and, therefore, to attach

any weight to the statement. In any event, she permitted Mr. Rivers frequent daytime contact with Joseph even during that period, and since then Mr. Rivers has had constant overnight access to him. He has even lived with Mr. Rivers and Ms. Cotton together on more than one occasion.

Nor does the evidence show that Mr. Rivers has had little interest in access. Mr. Rivers' access to Joseph has indeed been limited. He has had overnight access for only about 6 months and has lived with Joseph and Ms. Cotton for only about 19 months overall (a figure that assumes an error in line 5, paragraph 6 of Ms. Cotton's affidavit, which states 'winter of 1996' instead of 'winter of 1987'). Despite these limits, Mr. Rivers has always been fairly involved in Joseph's daily life. I therefore give no weight to Ms. Cotton's statement in her affidavit that in the past Mr. Rivers did not see his son on weekends. He spent a lot of time with Joseph during the week, and Ms. Cotton was able to spend time with him during her weekends off.

Sentences

PUNCTUATION *Exercises, p. 52*

1. Lastly, in this discourse on "fundamental justice," I wish to mention that the social and historical context in which this question is viewed should not be limited to common law or pre-*Charter* history.

Although some might argue for the omission of the first or both commas, I prefer to heighten the connection between "Lastly" and "I wish to mention."

2. Dr. John R. Lawson, Director of the Department of Legal Affairs, said that, in spite of the allegations, his Department would continue its present policy.

The second pair of commas illustrates the importance of separating parenthetical elements. If the commas are omitted, a momentary ambiguity appears: "in spite of the allegations his Department [made?]."

3. At this early stage in the development of the *Charter*, the principles of fundamental justice have not been fully explored.

4. Earlier last year, probably in response to the Commission's inquiry, the House of Commons, sitting in special session, enacted the recommended legislation.

5. In my opinion the primary test should be a practical one based on the only valid justification for the rule against duplicity: does the accused know the case he has to meet, or is he prejudiced in the preparation of his defence by ambiguity in the charge?

6. In this doctrine it is not up to the prosecution to prove negligence; instead, it is open to the defendant to prove that all due care has been taken.

7. The present case concerns the interpretation of two troublesome words frequently found in public welfare statutes: "cause" and "effect."

8. A homeowner who pays a fee for the collection of his garbage by a business which services the area could probably not be said to have caused or permitted the pollution if the collector dumps the garbage in the river.

No punctuation necessary. Were you paying attention? I know, the sentence is unwieldy, but commas will not help.

9. In this case the father has demonstrated his ability to provide for his son's material welfare, but he has not demonstrated his ability to provide a supportive home environment.

Notice that we omit the comma if we omit the word "he."

10. The applicants seek to quash those decisions on the grounds that they were denied a fair hearing; that they were not given enough information concerning the reasons for the transfer in order to be able to respond to those reasons adequately; that their submissions were not considered in any meaningful way by the Deputy Commissioner; and that the decisions were biased.

The lack of commas within commas makes it possible to use commas here rather than semicolons. I prefer the latter, however, because of the length of the clauses.

11. It is trite law that safeguards pertaining to prosecution for a criminal offence do not pertain to prison management decisions; the Warden, for example, did not need to be satisfied beyond a reasonable doubt that the plot existed.

The semicolon could be replaced by a period, but the phrase "for example" highlights the close logical connection between the two ideas.

12. On the date in question her counsel presented three witnesses: Dr. George Sims, a surgeon who has known the defendant for fourteen years; Michael Walsh, an addictions counsellor at the Summerville Treatment Centre who treated the defendant for six months; and Heather Wong, who has been a friend of the defendant's family for many years.

13. Fear of punishment, then, is but one factor to be considered in evaluating sincerity.

14. The regulations were not followed in this case, and the applicant's grievance was dealt with by the Commissioner at an inappropriate time.

15. In some situations, even though bias or a reasonable apprehension of bias may be said to exist, a decision will still be upheld on the grounds of necessity.

16. In deciding which of these two options is in Lester's best interests, I must weigh the enumerated criteria found in sections 65(1) and 37(3) of the *Child and Family Services Act* (C.F.C.A.), keeping in mind the principles that govern these sections.

17. Parliament has not mandated a minimum term of imprisonment but has left the appropriate penalty to the discretion of the trial court.

Another trick—no punctuation necessary. It might be helpful to consider some possible variations on this sentence. The original understates Parliament's action, treating it as a mere matter of fact. The revisions below gradually increase the emphasis on Parliament's action, culminating in version "c," which implies raised eyebrows:

> *a. Parliament has not mandated a minimum term of imprisonment, but it has left the appropriate penalty to the discretion of the trial court.*
>
> *b. Parliament has not mandated a minimum term of imprisonment; it has left the appropriate penalty to the discretion of the trial court.*
>
> *c. Parliament has not mandated a minimum term of imprisonment. Parliament has left the appropriate penalty to the discretion of the trial court.*

Small changes in punctuation and word choice can produce significant changes in effect.

18. At the site the police found the following weapons: two shotguns, one revolver, three hunting knives, and a .22 calibre rifle.

No need for semicolons here.

19. Mr. Jones is an alcoholic; the evidence is clear in that regard.

A dash is also possible and would heighten the dramatic effect.

20. Disrupting Carol's sleep at night, failing to provide her with adequate meals, arguing violently in her presence—these are not actions that recommend continued custody.

In the nineteenth century, the choice would have been the colon. Twentieth-century customs are less formal.

WORDINESS *Exercises, p. 56*

Savings are indicated parenthetically.

1. The facts now become murky. *(55%)*

2. The Hydro workers concluded at trial that burn marks on the primary power line and the backhoe proved that the Appellants themselves had caused the power outage. *(23%)*

3. This is not to suggest that large quantities of "activated sludge" could not harm the river. *(38%)*

4. The Crown states that the tape is lost. *(38%)*

5. Accordingly, a *de facto* assessment of the relationship between the accused and the complainants is appropriate; such an assessment warrants committal on the s. 153 charges. *(40%)*

6. The mother brings this application because the father canceled so many of his weekends with Sarah. *(33%)*

7. Mr. Harris's evidence is inconclusive. *(74%)*

8. According to the membership contract, the country club would revoke all privileges if Mr. Mesky missed more than two consecutive payments. *(30%)*

9. Is regular supervision by his grandparents in Giles's best interests? *(68%)*

10. Although the officer erred in his description, an approved instrument was used; both the subjective and objective tests set out in *Regina v. Storrey* have therefore been met. *(49%)*

SENTENCE STRUCTURE *Exercises, p. 62*

1. The police officer's belief that medical staff would have obtained a sample of the driver's blood for medical purposes is reasonable, given the circumstances: the end-over-end motor vehicle accident, the removal of the driver by emergency personnel, the odour of alcohol on the driver's breath, and the presence of alcohol bottles at the scene.

2. I make this conclusion for three reasons: Mr. Loris testified that he left the defendant's vehicle to travel in another vehicle in search of alcohol; Mr. Loris made no statement that he took the keys; and the defendant admitted that he retrieved the keys from the police.

3. He argues that due diligence does not preclude depositing waste into the water; it means minimizing the impact of the waste in a reasonable manner by following the guidelines.

4. Three issues remained: who should have custody of the children, what sum should be paid for their maintenance, and how should the matrimonial property be divided.

5. Counsel for the accused, Mr. Seresa, argued that the charge should have been theft by conversion, not theft, and that Custom Home Design's ownership of the property had not been proved beyond a reasonable doubt.

6. Her teacher claims that since her mother has begun her new job Carol's attendance has been irregular, she has had difficulty relating with her classmates, and, most importantly, she has neglected her work.

7. In claims of breach of either common law or fiduciary care, counsel for big corporations usually try to focus the attention of the court not on the responsibility of the corporation for the particular matter but on that of the employee who deals with it.

8. If counsel is necessary for individuals asked to sign documents risking their last penny on an apparently reasonable project, then counsel is surely necessary when a company's affairs may not be viable.

9. On this issue I do not find Walter Tolley a credible witness. I therefore reject his evidence that he did not participate in the sale or negotiation of the sale of the property, and that he received a cheque of one-thousand dollars payable to him, cashed the cheque, and gave the total amount to Mr. Rice.

10. The thrust of the legislative response to this problem is to discourage potential offenders by increasing both the likelihood of detection and the severity of the sanction.

Chapter 5: Words

The original sentences are provided first with the offending words underlined. The originals are then revised accordingly.

1. The argument as applied by counsel to the <u>instant</u> case is, <u>in essence</u>, that <u>prior to</u> and at the time of the rezoning application the nature of the project was clearly understood to be a condominium development.

Revision: Counsel argues in this case that both before and at the time of the rezoning application the project was clearly understood to be a condominium development.

2. In those Orders the <u>Learned</u> Master granted a Rice Order in the <u>within</u> foreclosure Action which, *inter alia*, approved the offer to purchase of the Appellant for the mortgaged property.

Revision: Within those Orders, the Master granted a Rice Order in the foreclosure Action, approving the Appellant's offer to purchase the mortgaged property.

3. <u>Prior to</u> May of 1988, Dynatech became dissatisfied with the performance of its <u>then</u> distributor.

Revision: Before May of 1988, Dynatech became dissatisfied with the performance of its distributor.

4. The Crown <u>advises</u> this Court that the tape has <u>in fact</u> been lost.

Revision: The Crown informs this Court that the tape has been lost.

5. The defence <u>has made an application</u> based on *Stinchcombe v. The Queen*, and <u>it is for</u> a stay of proceedings on the grounds of <u>failure on the part of the Crown</u> to provide full disclosure.

Revision: Relying on *Stinchcombe v. The Queen*, the defence applies for a stay of proceedings because the Crown failed to provide full disclosure.

6. However, in the event that <u>there is a non-compliance</u> with the conditions attached to the probation order, <u>recourse is possible</u> to S.26 Y.O.A. for a new breach charge.

Revision: However, if the probation order is violated, Section 26 of the Y.O.A. enables a new breach charge.

7. The diagnosis that the mother reported <u>had been determined</u> by the attending physician, <u>was that</u> the child had sustained a spiral fracture of the leg, resulting from an unexplained injury.

Revision: The mother reported that the attending physician had diagnosed a spiral fracture of the child's leg, resulting from an unexplained injury.

8. The meaning of <u>said</u> clause is fully explained in *Lassum v. The Queen* (<u>*supra*</u>, p.5).

Revision: The meaning of the clause is fully explained in *Lassum v. The Queen* (above, p.5).

9. The question is whether Star Brewery Ltd. (<u>hereinafter referred to as</u> "<u>Star</u>") took steps to avert the pollution of the stream.

Revision: The question is whether Star Brewery Ltd. (Star) took steps to avert the pollution of the stream.

10. The <u>instant</u> case, however, can be distinguished from *Payne v. The Queen*.

Revision: This case [*or* the present case], however, can be distinguished from *Payne v. The Queen*.

PREJUDICIAL LANGUAGE *Exercises, p. 73*

1. He was among a number of Inuit who graduated in 1967 from the University of Toronto.

2. Counsel argues that the claims of Jonathan's natural father to custody should outweigh those of his adoptive father.

3. There is no question that he contributed to the problem by acting in a stereotypically feminine manner. (*Or, one may specify the behaviour*).

4. Contemporary judges will know how to approach these questions. They will be trained in the relevant branches of the law, and they will be alert to their social implications.

5. The spokesperson for the Police Department explained that juvenile delinquency had increased dramatically along with the increase in wives who worked outside the home.

6. The aboriginal peoples living in Northern British Columbia have been pressing their claims for self-government. (*Or, better, name the specific peoples*).

7. Throughout history, humans have shown themselves to be innately litigious. (*Some might argue that the original version of this sentence is more accurate*).

8. When a lawyer makes such a statement in court, he or she can almost certainly count on an objection from the other side. (*Or use the plural*).

9. The bus line does not acknowledge that people with disabilities should receive assistance from drivers.

10. Once the men were tied up, the accused told the women to leave the room. (*Or,* Once the gentlemen were tied up, the accused told the ladies to leave the room.)

Chapter 6: Judicial Styles
Exercises, p. 84

1. Denning

In almost all cases a customer who signs a bank guarantee or a charge is bound by it. Any agreement made in ordinary circumstances cannot be altered. Many people suffer by this rule. A poor man who is homeless, for example, may agree to pay a high rent to a landlord simply to have shelter. In such a case the common law will not interfere, and any corrective action must come from Parliament. A borrower in urgent need of money, to take another example, may borrow from a bank at high interest with the guarantee of a friend. If the borrower cannot repay the loan and the friend has given his bond, the friend will be held responsible. In such a case, too, the common law will do nothing. Parliament is also unlikely to assist. Although Parliament has intervened to prevent moneylenders from charging excessive interest, it has never interfered with banks. (*152 words*)

This exercise enhanced my appreciation of Lord Denning. My version of the plain style is serviceable but uninspired. It lacks the vividness of Lord Denning's language, the crispness of his sentences, and the wit. Some might prefer the transparency of the plain style, however, to the self-conscious artfulness of the original.

2. Dickson

Each of these tests is beneficial within limits, but, as is illustrated by the variety of cases and the diversity of opinion in this case itself, each of them is too general to provide a clear demarcation in concrete instances. To resolve the matter one must recall the policy basis of the rule against multiplicity and duplicity, a rule that developed during a period of extreme formality and technicality in the preferring of indictments and laying of informations, and grew from the humane desire of Judges to alleviate the severity of the law in an age when many crimes were still classified as felonies, for which the punishment was death by the gallows. In that age the slightest defect made an indictment a nullity. That age, however, is no more. As Parliament has made abundantly clear, in those sections of the *Criminal*

Code pertaining to the form of indictments and informations, we must no longer be bound by the punctilio of an earlier age; we must seek not for petty formalities but for substance. *(174 words)*

As this revision illustrates, Chief Justice Dickson's formal style needs only slight changes in sentence length, structure, and word choice to become magisterial.

3. (a) A Formal Approach

The issue before the Court is whether Joan's best interests demand the continuing custody of the Society, a condition that would be achieved through an order of Crown wardship without access and would lead to the possible consequence of adoption, or whether they demand a return to the care of her father.

A status review application requires that Joan's best interests be determined by weighing the criteria enumerated in two sections of the *Child and Family Services Act* (C.F.S.A.): section 65(1), which deals with status review, and section 37(3), which deals with the best interests test. In weighing these criteria, the Court must consider the principles enunciated in section 1 of the C.F.S.A., and in particular the principle that, unless the best interests of the child are put in jeopardy, the integrity of the family must be respected and the unity of the family maintained. The legal validity of this test for status review applications was recently confirmed in the Supreme Court of Canada decision, *Catholic Children's Aid Society of Metropolitan Toronto v. Cidalia M. (185 words)*

(b) An Informal Approach

The question before me is which of two actions is most likely to achieve Joan's best interests. Should I order Crown wardship without access, an action that will keep her in the custody of the Society and may lead to her adoption? Or should I order a return to the care of her father?

To answer these questions, I must turn to the *Child and Family Services Act* (C.F.S.A.). I must first consider the declaration of principles in section 1 of the C.F.S.A., particularly those set out in sections 1(a) and (b). Those sections stress the need to respect the integrity of the family and to keep the unit intact unless to do so would not be in the best interests of the child. Having considered those principles, I must then weigh the criteria found in two sections: those on status review (65[1]), and those on best interests (37[3]). A recent decision of the Supreme Court of Canada, *Catholic Children's Aid Society of Metropolitan Toronto v. Cidalia M.*, recognizes this legislative test. *(181 words)*

A Reading List

Writer's Guide

William Strunk, Jr. and E. B. White, *The Elements of Style* (New York: Macmillan, 1979)

(The classic)

Dictionaries

The American Heritage Dictionary

The Concise Oxford Dictionary of Current English

The Gage Canadian Dictionary

The Canadian Oxford Dictionary

(Many good dictionaries are available, in English and French)

Handbook of Grammar and Usage

William E. Messenger and Jan de Bruyn, *The Canadian Writer's Handbook*, 3rd ed. (Scarborough, Ontario: Prentice-Hall, 1995)

(A reference work that includes the basic rules, with examples. Dozens of such handbooks exist; most are acceptable)

Usage and Editing

R. W. Burchfield, ed., *Fowler's Modern English Usage* (Oxford: Clarendon Press, 1996)

(The classic. Alphabetized entries on a host of debatable topics, including obsolete commas, acceptable danglers, the use of "gift" as a verb, and the difference between "proved" and "proven")

The Canadian Style: A Guide to Writing and Editing (Toronto: Dundurn Press, 1997)

(A standard reference work for government offices. Includes punctuation, spelling, abbreviations, gender bias, and more)

Margery Fee and Janice McAlpine, *Guide to Canadian English Usage* (Toronto: Oxford University Press, 1997)

(An excellent complement to Burchfield and Fowler)

Bob Taylor, ed., *The Canadian Press Stylebook* (Toronto: The Canadian Press, 1999)

(A guide for the Canadian Press. Alphabetized entries that include such things as age, business, government, names, race, technical terms, and spelling)

Legal Writing

Norman Brand and John O. White, *Legal Writing: The Strategy of Persuasion*, 3rd ed. (New York: St. Martin's Press, 1994)

Ronald Goldfarb and James C. Raymond, *Clear Understandings: A Guide to Legal Writing* (New York: Random House, 1982)

Roman N. Komar, *Reasons for Judgment* (Toronto: Butterworths, 1980)

Louise Mailhot and James D. Carnwath, *Decisions, Decisions: A Handbook for Judicial Writing* (Cowansville, Quebec: Les Éditions Yvon Blais, 1998)

Richard C. Wydick, *Plain English for Lawyers* (Carolina Academic Press, 1994)

(Useful guides to legal and judicial writing)

Gender Bias

Ruth King, *Talking Gender* (Toronto: Copp Clark Pitman, 1991)

(A helpful Canadian guide to gender bias. Includes French)

Style

Francis-Noël Thomas and Mark Turner, *Clear and Simple as the Truth* (Princeton: Princeton University Press, 1994)

(A sophisticated definition of "classic" prose style)

Joseph W. Williams, *Style: Toward Clarity and Grace* (Chicago: University of Chicago Press, 1990)

(An excellent book for advanced writers)

Miscellaneous

Orwell, George. "Politics and the English Language," in *Shooting an Elephant and Other Essays* (1945)

(A classic statement of the social and political importance of language)